W9-COI-379

BLACK AMERICA

BLA
AME

ACK
RICA

A Photographic Journey: Past to Present

Marcia A. Smith

THUNDER BAY
P·R·E·S·S
San Diego, California

Thunder Bay Press
An imprint of the Advantage Publishers Group
5880 Oberlin Drive, San Diego, CA 92121-4794
www.thunderbaybooks.com

ISBN 1-57145-872-7
Library of Congress Cataloging-in-Publication Data available upon request.

Printed in Singapore
1 2 3 4 5 06 05 04 03 02

(Title page) A pick-up baseball team with the barefoot boys wearing new hats and cast-off clothing, 1890s. (Overleaf) One of New York's Finest tearfully and proudly saluting fallen comrades, September 15, 2001.

Contents

JAMES

Introduction

An eighteenth-century British impression of West African costume, accoutrements, and weaponry—almost certainly fanciful since the artist would never have been there.

We black folk, our history and our present being,
are a mirror of all the manifold experiences of America.
What we want, what we represent, what we endure
is what America is. If we black folk perish,
America will perish.

Richard Wright, *12 Million Black Voices,* 1941

Africans arrived in what would become America speaking a multitude of languages, holding a range of beliefs, and carrying the skills that had made their lives possible and given them joy. The brutality of the slave trade and the institution of slavery disrupted African families, political structures, and cultural patterns. Traders and planters made it a practice to mix together slaves from many groups—both as a defense against the possibility of rebellions and to force Africans to speak to them, and one another, in European languages. The creation of an African American identity, so taken for granted today, was a gradual process. Not only did early New World blacks not consider themselves African American, they didn't think of themselves as African. They were Fulani, Ibo, Akan. But in America, Africans accomplished the great feat of re-creating themselves, and their identities, anew. Drawing on the skills, cultural practices, and beliefs they carried on the slave ships, adding experience acquired in the Americas, black people, incredibly, managed to survive and flourish. African Americans have made an indelible imprint on the United States, and over the centuries forged a unique culture and identity that continues to have a powerful worldwide impact.

This book tells part of their story through a collection of images—primarily photographs, with some engravings and drawings. The story told in these pages is by necessity an incomplete one; African Americans were not, for much of their history, in control of their own images. But look at these pictures, then take another look, then another. They have stories to tell. Look, and they may tell you how African Americans shaped their own destiny, grasping whatever power was within their control, and what lessons and stories they wanted to leave their children.

They show African Americans in possession of the full range of complex emotions and characteristics—heroic to cowardly, joyous to miserable, wretched to triumphant. The theme of these images, and the collective narrative of African Americans, is the struggle to make the United States live up to its promise of democracy and equality for all.

In August 1619, a Dutch man-of-war sailed into Point Comfort at Jamestown, in the New World colony of Virginia. The crew, which had seized the cargo of a Spanish ship, was hungry and haggard; they were anxious to find supplies and be on to the next leg of their voyage. Among the precious cargo aboard the Dutch ship were twenty Africans.

TO BE SOLD, on board the Ship *Bance-Island*, on tuesday the 6th of *May* next, at *Ashley-Ferry*; a choice cargo of about 250 fine healthy

NEGROES,

just arrived from the Windward & Rice Coast. —The utmost care has already been taken, and shall be continued, to keep them free from the least danger of being infected with the SMALL-POX, no boat having been on board, and all other communication with people from *Charles-Town* prevented.

Austin, Laurens, & Appleby.

N. B. Full one Half of the above Negroes have had the SMALL-POX in their own Country.

Advertisement for the sale of a cargo of slaves from the ship *Bante Island* in Boston, c. 1700.

A brief eighteenth-century exposition on the peoples of Africa.

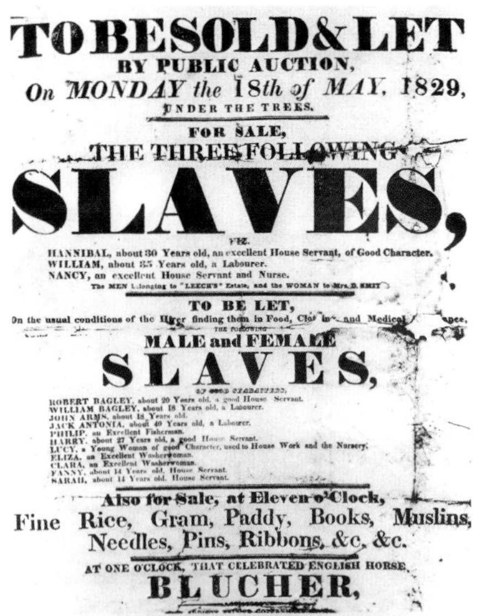

An advertisement for the sale and "letting," or leasing, of slaves in the West Indies, 1829.

They were not the first Africans to have traveled to the New World; others, over the previous hundred years, had come with Europeans as explorers, servants, or slaves. Thirty were with Balboa when he discovered the Pacific Ocean; several went into Mexico with Cortes; one, known as Esteban, is credited with opening up New Mexico and Arizona for the Spanish. But the Africans who landed at Jamestown in 1619 were the first black inhabitants of England's first stable colony in the Americas and probably the first to assume that they would live out their lives in this strange new world.

They were not, strictly speaking, slaves. The colony of Virginia had relied on the work of indentured servants, poor English natives who traded between four and seven years of their labor for passage to the colonies and a chance of freedom and prosperity at the end of their service. The Africans of 1619 were treated similarly; most of them would have been considered as any other indentured servant. But as tobacco cultivation in Virginia burgeoned and conditions at home in England restricted the number of indentured servants coming from there, the English colonists began to look for a new labor supply—labor that would be cheap and reliable. They turned first to the native peoples of their New World, enslaving many by force. But the Native Americans were on their home ground, knew the terrain, and were organized into societies that had the potential to resist. Desperate to build a predictable and compliant workforce, fatefully the colonists began to look south, to the example set by Europeans who had successfully established another system of labor on the islands of the Caribbean: African slavery. Over the next few decades, slowly but steadily, laws in Virginia and other colonies would restrict the freedom and status

Africans being taken down to the coast to be sold as slaves to European traders and then shipped to the Americas.

of Africans. By 1640, some Africans would be deemed servants for life; by 1662, newborn children would not automatically be free, but would assume the status of their mothers; and by 1694, a comprehensive slave code was put in place to define their status. By 1705, the Virginia General Assembly declared that "All servants imported and brought into the Country...who were not Christians in their native Country...shall be accounted and be slaves. All Negro, mulatto, and Indian slaves within this dominion...shall be held to be real estate. If any slave resists his master...correcting such slave, and shall happen to be killed in such correction...the master shall be free of all punishment...as if such accident never happened." From the 1660s, slavery based on race was introduced and legalized throughout the colonies of North America. The "terrible transformation" was complete.

Toussaint L'Ouverture, whose forces freed all Haiti's slave population and drove out the Europeans by 1794.

The North American colonies were hardly unique in sanctioning slavery; it had existed in both Europe and Africa for centuries. But such enslavement was based on tribal, religious, or class differences rather than race, and was not always lifelong or passed on to the next generation. European slavery of Africans, however, was already an accepted practice by the time the Dutch frigate arrived in Jamestown. A Portuguese sailor had captured twelve African slaves and presented them to the court in Lisbon as early as 1441. By 1700, slavery was well established in the Caribbean and South America, and the Spanish, the Portuguese, the French, and the Dutch were involved in a bustling trade in African slaves.

Haitian free ladies of color in 1791, the year when violence first broke out between the white planters and the people of color there, to be followed by a full-scale slave rebellion.

COSTUMES
DES AFFRANCHIES ET DES ESCLAVES
des Colonies.

European powers came to rely on what became known as the "triangle trade." For the first leg, ships left Europe for the west coast of Africa loaded with guns, ammunition, and other goods

A quadroon, or a quarter-black, slave in Surinam, the Dutch colony in South America, 1794.

to trade with African partners. In Africa, the ships would be outfitted with slave decks, and take on their human cargo of 300–700 people. Then came the horror of the Middle Passage, as the trip across the Atlantic to the New World became known, followed by the sale of those Africans who survived to white settlers in the colonies of the Caribbean and North America. Finally, the ships loaded raw materials produced in the colonies to feed Europe's growing appetite for luxury goods—sugar, tobacco, and cotton—and sailed back to Europe. In time, the triangle trade would be supplemented by slaving voyages directly to Africa from the Americas.

The Middle Passage was one of the greatest human barbarities imaginable. A typical voyage across the Atlantic took between two and three months, with some lasting as long as four. The captives were packed shoulder to shoulder into cramped spaces on ships specially modified to carry the greatest possible number of human beings. They were often shackled together—the living sometimes chained to the dead—and subject to starvation, thirst, illness, and brutality. If they survived, they merely faced a lifetime of hardship, as did their descendants. But millions did not survive the Middle Passage and instead succumbed to disease or hunger, or died at the hands of their captors. In desperation, some committed suicide or threw newborn babies overboard, leaving a trail of bones and tears across the Atlantic.

> The closeness of the place, and the heat of the climate, added to the number in the ship, which was so crowded that each had scarcely room to turn himself, almost suffocated us.... This wretched situation was aggravated by the falling of the chains, now become

> insupportable; and the filth of the necessary tubs, into which the children often fell, and were almost suffocated. The shrieks of the women and the groans of the dying rendered the whole a scene of horror almost inconceivable.... Two of my wearied countrymen who were chained together...preferred death to such a life of misery, somehow made through the nettings and jumped into the sea.
>
> Olaudah Equiano, 1789

Brazilian slaves wait on their master and their mistress, who entertains herself with two slave children.

The first to be enslaved were captured directly by Europeans, but Africans soon became involved. Up and down the west coast of Africa, European merchants established forts and trading posts known as "slave castles" to serve as command centers and staging areas. With gunpowder, liquor, and other commodities, the Europeans developed African trading partners to act as their agents. War, famine, political instability, and other disputes among the diverse African ethnic groups fed the flow of slaves to the coast from as far as 1,000 miles inland.

Between eleven and twenty million Africans were torn from their homelands in the slave trade; as many as ten percent did not survive the Middle Passage. No one knows how many people died in Africa during wars to sieze captives, in the forced march to the shore, or in the coast forts and holding pens where slaves awaited their departure for the New World. The great majority of captive Africans were sent to Latin America and the Caribbean, with only five to six percent ending up in what is today the United States. If they survived the passage, Africans found more misery awaiting them: They were washed and oiled, paraded, and branded with hot irons; families who had managed

Nat Turner's Rebellion, Virginia, 1831—the most significant of all the slave revolts.

to stay together were deliberately separated, as were Africans who spoke the same language. They were sold at auction and put to work at a variety of tasks, from clearing forests to cooking, to trapping.

Slaves could be found throughout the colonies. But in the north, where the development of plantation farming was inhibited by the cooler climate, smaller numbers of slaves could be put to work. It was large-scale agriculture in the southern colonies that required the most labor, and thus it was there that the majority of Africans were deployed. By the middle of the eighteenth century, over ninety percent of American slaves lived in the South. Their labor was the backbone of the growing southern economy, while the northern colonies were in some measure dependent on them, too, directly or indirectly. And some prominent Northerners and northern institutions profited directly from the slave trade. Nicholas and John Brown, two of the founders of what became Brown University, were slave traders; Harvard Law School was endowed with money its founder earned from selling slaves for Antigua's cane fields; and Yale University relied on slave trading profits for its first scholarships, endowed professorships, and library endowments.

Africans expressed their discontent through a variety of means. Two hundred and fifty shipboard revolts by slaves have been documented, and 250 more violent incidents were initiated by slaves on land. These mass uprisings were, of course, in addition to frequent and widespread individual acts of defiance. The most significant slave revolt of the colonial era took place in 1739 in South Carolina, where Africans outnumbered whites by two to one. On a Sunday morning as their masters went to church, a group of slaves gathered along the banks of the Stono River, near Charleston. After breaking into a firearms store and seizing weapons, they raided and set fire to the plantations lining the river, killing twenty-five white men, women, and children. The Stono Rebellion was quickly put down by white soldiers, who outnumbered and outgunned the slaves. The heads of the more than forty slaves subsequently executed were displayed on mileposts throughout the Charleston area.

The Stono Rebellion, like other uprisings that occurred sporadically throughout the years, had little chance of success, whatever the hopes they inspired among slaves. They certainly provoked near panic among slaveholders throughout the southern colonies. In their wake, planters often implemented more repressive measures. South Carolina's 1740 slave code, for example, made it legal to kill a slave who was discovered away from his or her owner's property. Fifteen years later, Georgia's code actually encouraged the murder of adult male runaways. The reward for returning a dead male slave was twice the amount offered for returning a woman or child who was still alive. Still, enslaved people continued to plan and carry out rebellions, the best known of which are those organized by Gabriel Prosser in 1800, Denmark Vesey in 1822, and Nat Turner in 1831. These, too, were to be followed by the enactment of more repressive measures.

As the American Revolution got under way, slavery was legal in all thirteen colonies and slaves constituted about forty percent of the population of the southern mainland colonies. As they did in every subsequent military conflict, African Americans seized the opportunities created by the war to press for their own

Crispus Attucks, killed by the British in the Boston Massacre, 1770.

liberation. For many colonists, the task of determining whether to swear loyalty to the British or to the idea of a new nation was a difficult one. But the self-interest of slaves demanded that they side with whomever would provide the best chance for freedom.

Blacks were involved from the first days of the conflict. In March of 1770, fifty Boston seamen gathered to protest the presence of British troops guarding British customs officers. Among them was Crispus Attucks, an escaped slave who made his living on whaling ships on the New England coast. When British soldiers fired on the protesters, Attucks was the first of five men killed in what became known as the Boston Massacre, thought of as the incident that sparked the American Revolution. The New England colonies of Connecticut, Massachusetts, and Rhode Island employed African Americans in their militias and in the Continental Army. In 1775, after the Battle of Bunker Hill, the Massachusetts legislature commended black militiaman Salem Poor, declaring that "in the person of this said Negro centers a brave and gallant soldier."

But when he took command of the Continental Army that year, George Washington barred the further recruitment of black soldiers. It wasn't until the winter of 1777, when disease and desertion had decimated the Continental Army and African Americans were being recruited by the British, that Washington approved plans for a black regiment. Ultimately, some 5,000 African Americans, slave and free, joined the Continental Army.

Many enslaved Africans, however, believed that a British victory was a surer route to freedom. Their instinct to side with the enemies of the slaveholders was lent weight when the British began to actively recruit slaves belonging to the colonists. In November of 1775, John Murray, Earl of Dunmore and royal governor of Virginia, issued a proclamation offering freedom to any slaves who would desert their colonist owners and join the British royal forces. Not only would widespread desertion of the plantations have a disastrous economic impact on the colonies, Dunmore reasoned, but it would feed the colonists' growing fear of armed slave revolts and turn their attention from the war with the British to defending their lives and property.

Dunmore's declaration swept through the slave community like lightning, leading hundreds to offer themselves at his doorstep even before the proclamation was formally issued. Three hundred blacks were quickly inducted into the "Ethiopian Regiment," armed and outfitted in military uniforms inscribed with the words "Liberty to Slaves."

What Africans found with the British military was less than equality. Often they were relegated to building roads and serving officers. But in places like New York, black men and women spied for the British and sabotaged the rebellious colonists' activities. As was also true of blacks who served with the American colonists, African Americans who served with the British military built networks and gained experience that would be put to use in the coming years to help enslaved people escape to freedom.

In response to the British recruitment drive, the colonial rebels stepped up tactics to prevent blacks from going over to them. They tried to pacify African Americans with promises of freedom, or at least fairer treatment: The *Virginia Gazette*

African Americans in Canada, 1859. They are probably escaped slaves earning a living as street musicians with their barrel organs and performing monkeys.

warned slaves: "Be not...tempted by the proclamation to ruin your selves," and urged them to "cling to their kind masters." But the colonists also tightened the screws of repression. Restrictions on slave meetings were strengthened, and Virginia declared that runaways to the British would be pardoned if they returned in ten days, but severely punished if they did not.

All told, an estimated 100,000 African American slaves took advantage of wartime disruption to escape bondage. Many fled to Canada, to Spanish Florida, or to Native American territories. Thomas Jefferson estimated that Virginia lost 30,000 slaves in one year alone. Of those who sided with the British, thousands of African Americans ended up losing their freedom again. Some left American shores only to be enslaved in the Caribbean. Some, like ex-slave Boston King, feared the future despite the end of the conflict: "Peace was restored between America and Great Britain, which diffused universal joy among all parties, except us, who had escaped from slavery, and taken refuge in the English army," he said, "for a report prevailed at New York, that all the slaves ...were to be delivered up to their masters."

In the new nation, the wartime rhetoric of freedom inspired a wave of manumission laws in the north. Vermont amended its constitution to ban slavery as early as 1777. Over the next twenty-five years, though some would stipulate gradual rather than immediate emancipation, every state north of the Delaware River would take steps to ban slavery: Pennsylvania in 1780, Massachusetts and New Hampshire in 1783, Connecticut and Rhode Island in 1784, New York in 1799, and New Jersey in 1804.

Southern slave-grown cotton was first exploited in the 1780s and soon became the nation's leading export, revolutionizing textile manufacturing in both New England and Europe, and stimulating banking, insurance, and shipping, as well as being highly influential in national politics. After the 1793 invention of the cotton gin led the productivity of slave labor to explode, the slave system became even more firmly entrenched. And the North, despite growing antislavery sentiment, continued to benefit economically as slave-produced raw materials drove production in the textile mills and southern planters purchased clothing for slaves from northern manufacturers. In 1800, slavery in America was a stronger institution than it had been at the start of the Revolutionary War.

Eli Whitney's cotton gin, which hugely increased the amount of cotton that one slave could clean in a day.

As the new nation approached its first Constitutional Convention, the issue of slavery loomed large. Southern delegates wanted to ensure that the Constitution did not deprive them of the right to continue to own slaves. In Virginia, for example, with a black majority in some counties, hundreds of signatures of whites were gathered to protest the "very subtle and daring attempt...to dispossess us of a very important Part of our Property, by an act of Legislature for general emancipation." As the Constitution was being drafted in the summer of 1787, among the most important questions was how states would be represented in the federal government of the new and ostensibly democratic country. Though African Americans were not considered people, much less citizens, white delegates to the Constitutional Convention demanded, and won, a compromise allowing the inclusion of the slave population in the calculation of the number of representatives for each state. In states allowing slavery, for the purposes of representation in the House of

A

THANKSGIVING SERMON,

PREACHED JANUARY 1, 1808,

In St. Thomas's, or the African Episcopal, Church, Philadelphia:

ON ACCOUNT OF

THE ABOLITION

OF THE

AFRICAN SLAVE TRADE,

ON THAT DAY,

BY THE CONGRESS OF THE UNITED STATES.

BY ABSALOM JONES,

RECTOR OF THE SAID CHURCH.

PHILADELPHIA:

PRINTED FOR THE USE OF THE CONGREGATION.

FRY AND KAMMERER, PRINTERS.

1808.

2

Title page of printed version of a sermon preached in the African Episcopal Church, Philadelphia, 1808, giving thanks for abolition.

Representatives, slaves would be counted as three-fifths of a person.

The three-fifths rule gave slave-owning a political value in addition to its economic one; it was another incentive for southern states to import slaves, even when the international trade became illegal in 1808. In addition, the disproportionate power of southern slave states allowed them to dominate national politics from the founding of the Union to the Civil War.

Though some of the Founding Fathers, including George Washington and Thomas Jefferson, would voice private concern about the morality of slavery, most were themselves slave owners, as were eight of the first twelve presidents. Other than Jefferson's and Madison's opposition to the transatlantic slave trade—they did not oppose the interstate trade—no chief executive between Washington and Lincoln took public action against slavery.

One of the greatest threats to the system of slavery, many whites believed, was the growing presence of free African Americans. According to the 1790 census, there were 59,000 free blacks in the United States—about 27,000 in the North and 32,000 in the South. The total number of free blacks would rise to nearly 320,000 over the next forty years. In addition to providing living proof of black intellectual equality, proslavery whites feared that free blacks might inspire restlessness and ambition among slaves, and might use their wealth in the service of emancipation.

Indeed, free African Americans did form vibrant communities in many parts of the country, including Philadelphia, Boston, and New York in the north, and New Orleans in the south. Many free blacks were poor, and the lives of all were circumscribed by exclusion and discrimination, but among them were skilled workers, entrepreneurs, and professionals who bought land and built businesses. Free African Americans played a key role in the development of a range of institutions. By 1787 there were black branches of the Baptist, Methodist, Presbyterian, and Episcopalian churches; by 1796 the independent black denominations of the African Methodist Episcopal and the African Methodist Episcopal Zion churches had been created. The African Free School, founded in New York City in 1787, offered primary education to black New Yorkers for almost fifty years. And free blacks organized mutual aid societies, black fraternal and charitable groups, and other organizations that in the years to come became very important in the fight against slavery.

Phyllis Wheatley, the poet (1753–1784).

White intolerance of free blacks escalated with the growth of the free black population. In 1817, the Reverend Robert Finley, with the help of Elias B. Caldwell, Clerk of the Supreme Court, and Francis Scott Key, author of "The Star Spangled Banner," established the American Colonization Society (ACS) for the purposes of encouraging free blacks to leave the United States, after rejecting the idea of creating a black territory in the U.S. for fear that it would become a haven for runaway slaves. In 1821, after securing congressional support, the ACS purchased land along the West African Coast, the kernel of what would later become the nation of Liberia. The ACS, and the idea of emigration, would come to win popular white support, including that of Presidents Lincoln, Madison, and Monroe. In the words of Congressman Henry Clay, "Can there be a nobler

Ellen Craft, whose pale complexion allowed her to pass as a white man and flee to England with her husband as her "slave," c. 1845.

Captain Paul Cuffe, black Boston shipowner, businessman, Quaker, and advocate of the repatriation of blacks to Africa.

cause than that which, whilst it proposed to rid our country of a useless and pernicious, if not dangerous portion of its population, contemplates the spreading of the arts of civilized life, and the possible redemption from ignorance and barbarism of a benighted quarter of the globe!"

Free African Americans had mixed feelings about emigration. The wealthy black Massachusetts shipper Paul Cuffe believed that emigration to Africa offered African Americans a better chance for freedom and success than they would ever find on American soil. In 1815, Cuffe captained his own ship, with a black crew, to the port of Sierra Leone to relocate thirty-eight free black Americans there. This British settlement for ex-slaves in West Africa had been established in 1787. James Forten, a Philadelphia businessman, and African Methodist Episcopal Church founder Richard Allen, agreed that emigration to Africa was preferable to living in a country they believed would never really accept them as citizens. But when 3,000 black men packed a Philadelphia church to discuss it, the idea of emigration met with resounding disapproval. "We prefer being colonized in the most remote corner of the land of our nativity," they declared, "to being exiled to a foreign country.... Whereas our ancestors (not of choice) were the first cultivators of the wilds of America, we their descendents feel ourselves entitled to participate in the blessings of her luxuriant soil.... Resolved, that we never will separate ourselves voluntarily from the slave population in this country; they are our brethren by the ties of consanguinity, of suffering, and of wrongs." All told, an estimated 15,000 to 20,000 African Americans emigrated to West Africa during the early nineteenth century. But the increasingly vehement opposition of black leaders and communities to the idea of

A warning against kidnapping to the "colored people of Boston," after the passing of the Fugitive Slave Act.

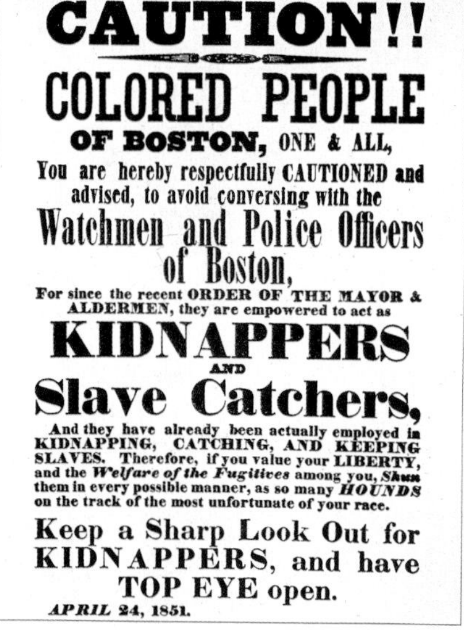

emigration gave impetus to white antislavery forces to break with the ACS, and eventually to found the American Anti-Slavery Society in 1833.

With growing abolitionism in the North and stubborn intransigence among slaveholders in the South, the United States was, by midcentury, well on its way to the sectional conflict that would engulf the nation later in the century.

AMERICAN
ANTI-SLAVERY
ALMANAC,
FOR
1840,

BEING BISSEXTILE OR LEAP-YEAR, AND THE 64TH OF AMERICAN INDEPENDENCE. CALCULATED FOR NEW YORK; ADAPTED TO THE NORTHERN AND MIDDLE STATES.

NORTHERN HOSPITALITY—NEW YORK NINE MONTHS' LAW.
The slave steps out of the slave-state, and his chains fall. A free state, with another chain, stands ready to re-enslave him.

Thus saith the Lord, Deliver him that is spoiled out of the hands of the oppressor.

NEW YORK:
PUBLISHED BY THE AMERICAN ANTI-SLAVERY SOCIETY,
NO. 143 NASSAU STREET.

The polarization of attitudes to slavery between North and South became clearer with the publications of journals like the *American Anti-Slavery Almanac*.

Blessed and behatted
Ladies waiting for a religious service in Woodville, Georgia, 1942.

One

Slavery and the Civil War 1850–1865

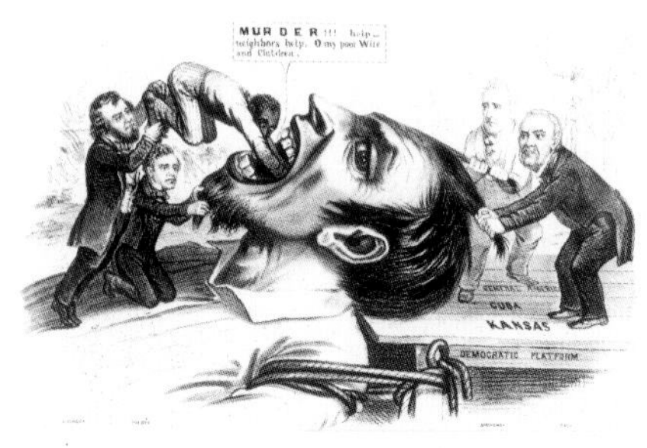

An 1856 cartoon of politicians forcing slavery down the throat of a "freesoiler," one of those opposed to the extension of slavery to the new western states.

Slavery was American original sin. African slaves were bought, traded, sold, insured, and advertised; like any other commodity, there was a price affixed to black flesh. In 1836, Franklin & Armfield, one of the largest slave-trading companies in the nation, placed the following advertisement in the *National Intelligencer* newspaper:

> Cash for five hundred negroes, including both sexes from ten to twenty five years of age. Persons having likely servants to dispose of, will find in their interest to give us a call, as we will give higher prices in cash than any other purchaser who is now or may hereafter come into the MARKET.

Michael Shiner, who was freed when his master died in 1832, came home from a job at the Washington Navy Yard six months later to find his wife and three children gone. They had been sold to Franklin & Armfield as slaves. Shiner wrote of the terror he felt before he was able to find, and then purchase, his family: "I went to great distress but never the less with the assistance of God I got my wife and children clear."

Slaves might work as house servants, carpenters, or trappers; they could be found in industries as diverse as construction, mining, and forest clearing. But most slaves were agricultural workers. In Maryland, Virginia, and North Carolina, slaves cultivated tobacco; in South Carolina and Georgia, rice. But when it came to reliance on large numbers of slaves, no crop compared to cotton. Comprising more than half the total value of domestic exports, cotton profits capitalized railroad construction, facilitated territorial expansion, and fueled industrialization.

Previous page
Escaped slaves, 1861. With the outbreak of the Civil War, thousands fled behind Union lines. Lincoln's policy was to return escaped slaves to their owners, as the federal law required, but General Butler, Union commander in Virginia, declared self-emancipated slaves "contraband," nonreturnable spoils of war.

All told, a million slaves were sold to the Deep South before 1860 to meet the burgeoning demand for labor. Charles Ball, who was sold away from his wife and children to work cotton in Georgia, wrote in 1836 about his first glimpse of plantation slavery.

> I observed that these poor people did not raise their heads...but kept their faces steadily bent towards the cotton-plants...I almost shuddered at the sight, knowing that I myself was doomed to a state of servitude equally cruel and debasing, unless, by some unforeseen occurrence, I might fall into the hands of a master of less inhumanity of temper than the one who had possession of the miserable creatures before me.

The 1850 Fugitive Slave Act meant constant danger for free African Americans, like these churchgoers in Cincinnati, Ohio, just across the Ohio River from the slaveholding state of Kentucky.

Out of view of their owners, slaves recognized and preserved their own humanity—loving, cooking, planting, fighting, praying, birthing and burying, laughing, and dreaming. But the system of slavery respected neither bonds of affection nor kinship. Marriages were not recognized; masters, rather than parents, had legal authority over slave children; and the threat of family separation through sale was ever-present. Slaves were subject to violence and cruelty at the whim of their masters. Frederick Douglass wrote in 1846:

> A mere look, word, or motion—a mistake, accident, or want of power—are all matters for which a slave may be whipped. Does a slave look dissatisfied? It is said, he has the devil in him, and it must be whipped out. Does he speak loudly when spoken to by his master? Then he is getting high-minded and should be taken down a button-hole lower. Does he forget to pull off his hat at the approach of a white person? Then he is wanting in reverence, and should be whipped for it. Does he ever venture to vindicate his conduct, when censured for it? Then he is guilty of impudence—one of the greatest crimes of which a slave can be guilty.

An 1853 advertisement seeking to buy slaves in Kentucky for sale in the New Orleans Market.

Slaves' resistance took many forms: from a feigned illness, a concocted difficulty using equipment, or foot-dragging, to poisoning or a full-scale revolt. But most often, slaves ran. About a thousand slaves per year ran away to the northern states or Canada. Ex-slave Charles Ball described a white overseer's frustration with slaves' persistence: "When I overseed for Colonel Polk," Ball quotes the man as saying, "he had two Yankee niggers that he brought from Maryland, and they were running away every day. I gave them a hundred lashes more than a dozen times; but they never quit running away, till I chained them together, with iron collars round their necks, and chained them to spades."

Henry "Box" Brown, packed into a three-foot-square wooden box, had himself shipped from Virginia to Philadelphia in 1849. After twenty-six hours inside, he was free.

The 1850 passage of the Fugitive Slave Act mandated federal action to return escaped slaves to their owners, prohibited runaways from testifying at their own trials, and instituted fines for private citizens who failed to comply with the law. It drastically expanded the power of slaveholders, and made all African Americans—slave or free—vulnerable.

Anthony Burns was a case in point. Burns had led a life of relative privilege: He supervised other slaves, belonged to a church, and knew how to read and write. His master, Charles Suttle of Alexandria, Virginia, even permitted him to hire himself out if he paid Suttle a fee. Still, Burns chafed under the strictures of bondage. "I began to hear about a North, and to feel the necessity for freedom of soul and body," he later said. "I heard of a North where men of my color could live without any man daring to say to them, 'You are my property'; and I determined by the blessing of God, one day to find my way there." In 1854, Anthony Burns struck out for freedom. While working for hire in Richmond, Burns secretly boarded a ship north to Boston.

The 54th Massachusetts Volunteer Infantry was the first authorized African-American regiment. In July 1863 it stormed Fort Wagner, South Carolina, losing nearly half its men and its commanding officer, Robert Gould Shaw, who was from a wealthy white abolitionist family.

After learning of Burns's whereabouts, Suttle invoked the 1850 Fugitive Slave Act and traveled to Boston to claim his "property." Burns was arrested and imprisoned in the federal courthouse. Black and white Boston abolitionists, outraged at the incursion of slave power on free land, rallied to Burns's defense and tried to force their way into the courthouse to free him. A deputy died in the ensuing melee, when the federal government intervened on the side of Burns's master. President Franklin Pierce activated 2,000 well-armed federal troops to quell any opposition to Burns's capture. An estimated 50,000 people lined the streets of Boston to witness Anthony Burns, once again in shackles, escorted to the dock where a federal ship waited to return him to slavery. Burns's story had a happier ending than those of many other fugitives. A black church raised $1,300 to purchase him, and in less than a year, he was back in Boston, a free man. Tensions between the North and the South escalated throughout the 1850s, and in 1860, the election of Abraham Lincoln set the stage for the simmering conflict to break out into the open. Though Lincoln was opposed to slavery, he was deeply ambivalent about using governmental authority to end it. At the outbreak of the Civil War in 1861, Lincoln's overriding goal was to preserve national unity. "If I could save the Union without freeing any slave," he said, "I would do it, and if I could save it by freeing all the slaves I would do it; and if I could save it by freeing some and leaving others alone I would also do that." But Lincoln later saw emancipation as a tactical necessity. Because slaves were critical to the southern economy, their emancipation would cripple the Confederacy's military capabilities.

Abraham Lincoln in Richmond, Virginia, shortly after it was captured by Union troops.

The Emancipation Proclamation signed by Lincoln declared that as of January 1, 1863, slaves in Confederate states not under Union control "shall be then, thenceforward, and forever free."

But many slaves had already taken matters into their own hands. With the first shots fired, thousands, like the families crossing the Rappahannock River on page 44, seized the opportunity to escape behind Union Army lines. President Abraham Lincoln's policy was to return escapees to their owners, as required under the Fugitive Slave Law. But a handful of Union generals declared self-emancipated slaves "contraband," spoils of war, and put them to work as cooks, builders, and scouts in Union-controlled territories.

Their work as contrabands was indispensable, but African Americans strained to become combatants in a war in which they had the biggest stake. Not until 1862 did Lincoln agree to place black troops under arms. Volunteers were organized into all-black units, including the 54th Massachusetts Volunteer Infantry, the 1st South Carolina Colored Volunteers, and the proud soldiers of the 4th U.S. Colored Infantry pictured on page 56.

Two of Frederick Douglass's sons served in the Army. One, Lewis, captured the passion and pride of black soldiers when he wrote to his sweetheart shortly after he was wounded in battle: "This regiment has established itself as a fighting regiment...not a man flinched, though it was a trying time," he said. "I wish we had a hundred thousand colored troops—we would put an end to this war."

THE
BOSTON SLAVE RIOT,
AND
TRIAL
OF
Anthony Burns,

CONTAINING THE
REPORT OF THE FANEUIL HALL MEETING; THE MURDER OF BACHELDER; THEODORE PARKER'S LESSON FOR THE DAY; SPEECHES OF COUNSEL ON BOTH SIDES, CORRECTED BY THEMSELVES; VERBATIM REPORT OF JUDGE LORING'S DECISION; AND, A DETAILED ACCOUNT OF THE EMBARKATION.

BOSTON:
FETRIDGE AND COMPANY.
1854.

Press of J. S. Potter & Co., 2 Spring Lane and 130 Washington Street.

In 1854 Anthony Burns fled to Boston. His master invoked the 1850 Fugitive Slave Act, so black and white abolitionists tried to free him by force, but his return to slavery was ensured by 2,000 troops. Some months later a black church raised the $1,300 to free him.

An upstanding business
Its solid brick construction connoting stability and integrity, this building in Alexandria, Virginia, had been the headquarters of Franklin & Armfield, one of the largest slave-trading companies. Price, Birch & Co succeeded Franklin & Armfield. In 1863, when this photo was taken, the building was used by the Union Army as a military prison, as barracks for "contrabands," and as a hospital for black soldiers.

PRICE, BIRCH & CO
DEALERS IN SLAVES.

King Cotton
Most slaves worked in agriculture: cultivating tobacco in Maryland, Virginia, and North Carolina, and rice in South Carolina and Georgia. Cotton, however, was the crop requiring the most labor, and was mostly grown in Alabama, Louisiana, and Mississippi. In 1791 American cotton production was just two million pounds. But by 1860, fueled by slave labor, the invention of the cotton gin, and worldwide demand, particularly from the mills of Lancashire in England, it had grown to a billion pounds. Cotton grew low to the ground, so workers could be easily seen and easily supervised by a white overseer on his horse.

Cruel and unusual punishment
Slaves were subject to violence and cruelty at the whim of their masters, who employed many devices of discipline. A shirtless slave stands with his hands tied to a whipping post as a white man begins the beating (right). The stocks and platform built above will wait for another slave, another day. Peter (far right) displays a patchwork of scars on his back in 1863, the result of a whipping by overseer Artayov Carier. "I was two months in bed, sore from my whipping. My master came after I was whipped; he discharged the overseer."

Slave family, South Carolina
The system of slavery respected neither bonds of affection nor kinship. Still, despite their tenuous status, families were slaves' best refuge from lives of hardship and instability.

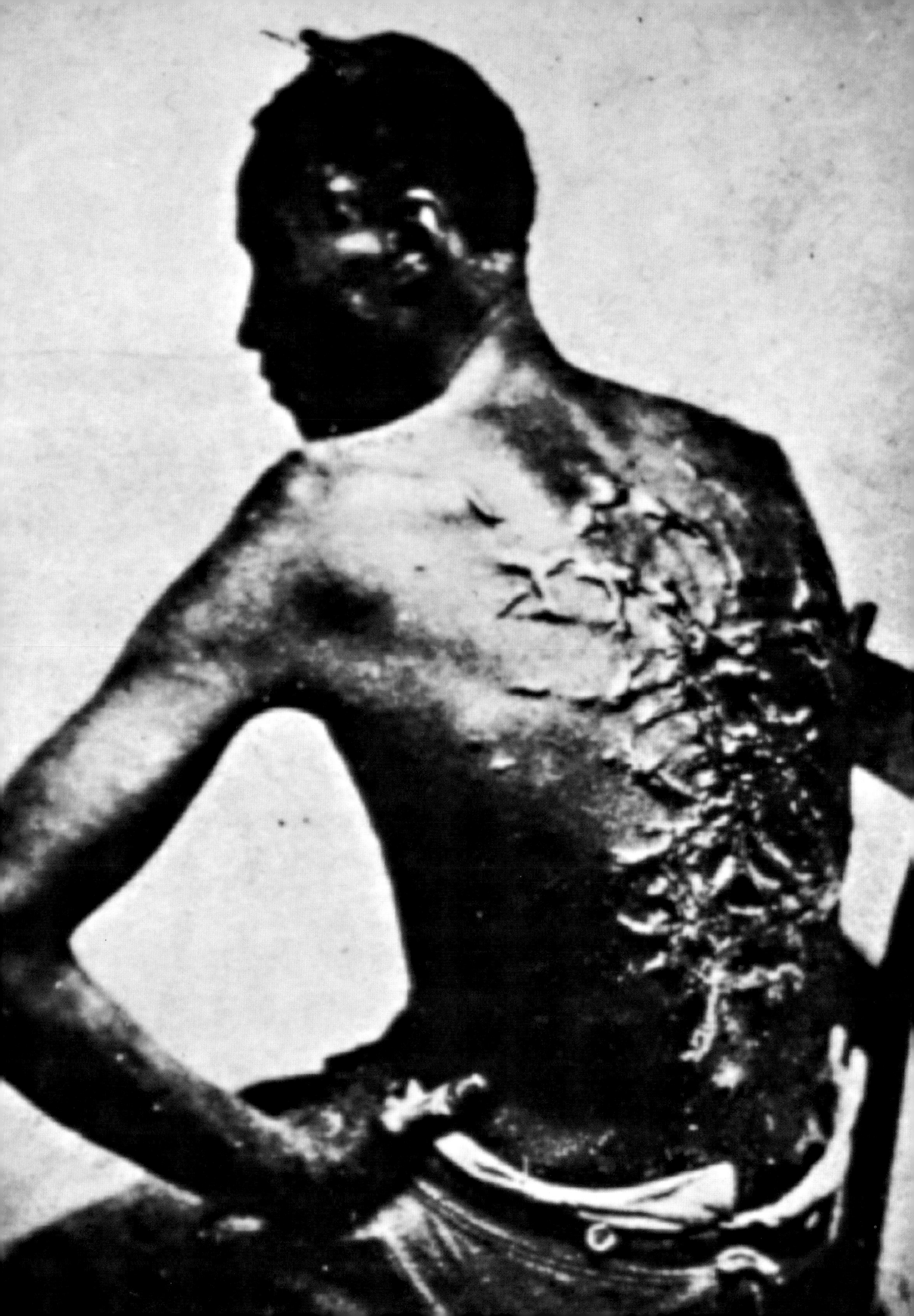

Abolitionists

Frederick Douglass (top left) escaped slavery in Maryland to become a leading abolitionist thinker, lecturer, publisher, and writer. William Lloyd Garrison (top right) founded *The Liberator*, a radical abolitionist paper, and cofounded the American Anti-Slavery Society. He and Douglass broke over his pacifism and rejection of politics. Activism in the political arena came from Senator Charles Sumner (bottom left). Dred Scott (bottom right) sued for his freedom and extracted an infamous ruling from the Supreme Court that blacks "might justly and lawfully be reduced to slavery," being "so far inferior that they had no rights that the white man was bound to respect." Harriet Tubman (right) was a legendary "conductor" on the Underground Railroad, a loose network that sheltered and guided runaway slaves northward. She admonished the fainthearted with the threat "Live North, or die here."

The Oberlin rescuers
In September 1858, John Price was kidnapped by Kentucky slave catchers in Oberlin, Ohio. When word reached Oberlin College, a center of abolitionist activism, a large crowd rushed the hotel where Price was being held, freed him, and whisked him off to Canada. Thirty-seven rescuers were arrested, two were convicted, and the others remained in jail out of solidarity. Immediately after their discharge from custody, the rescuers held a meeting at the Cuyahoga jail. They unanimously resolved to "hereafter, as we have heretofore, help the parting fugitive to escape from those who would enslave him, whatever may be the authority under which they may act."

John Quincy Adams (above), former president, defended the captives of the slave ship *Amistad*, who were on trial for murder and piracy after a bloody shipboard revolt. The Africans were freed to return to Sierra Leone. Sojourner Truth, (far right) born a slave in upstate New York about 1797, became one of the most prominent African-American women of her day and a champion of equal rights for blacks and women. Abraham Lincoln (right) was opposed to slavery, but deeply ambivalent about using government authority to end it. At the outbreak of the Civil War, his overriding goal was to preserve national unity, but by 1863, he saw emancipation as a tactical necessity, since without slaves the Confederacy's military capability would be crippled.

Rappahanock River, Virginia

By the thousands, they ran: the old and the young; men, women, and children; in small groups and large; in families or alone. They moved, carrying only what they could use. They hid quietly in the woods; one keeping watch ahead, one always looking behind. They slept in swamps and high grass, and woke before the light to move again. They ran—for the safety promised if they could just cross the river, just cross the bridge to reach the Union lines—free.

A game of poker

Confederate soldiers relax in a camp as African Americans look on. The Confederate Army used slaves as ditchdiggers, servants, laborers, and cooks, and in other support roles. Both armies relied on African Americans during the war, marginalized though they might have been.

At ease

Four Union soldiers outside their tents while an African American soldier serves food and drinks. For the Union Army, the bewildering numbers of escaped slaves posed logistical, moral, and political problems. Some self-liberated slaves, known as "contrabands," were put to work in support of the Union troops. As the war wore on, the Union permitted African Americans wider roles as combatants.

Burial party

A group of black men at the macabre task of burying the remains of the war dead at Cold Harbor, Virginia. Nearly 60,000 Union soldiers had been killed or wounded in the battles of Gaines Mill and Cold Harbor in June 1864.

Cock fighting

Though outlawed, cock fighting served as recreation in army camps, like the Union Army of the Potomac here, near the site of the Battle of Petersburg, in 1864. Two black men are readying cocks for a fight.

Crew

The U.S. Navy, unlike the Army, was never closed to African Americans, and at the start of the Civil War, blacks flocked to serve. Eighteen thousand African American men and more than a dozen women served in the Navy during the war, comprising fifteen percent of the total enlisted force. Eight black sailors earned the Medal of Honor for their heroism in battle. But segregation and subordination of black sailors prevailed onboard Navy ships. Black and white sailors on the deck of the *Hunchback* (right) served together in the waters off North Carolina and Virginia, and engaged Confederate forces on several occasions. But even recreational activities were carried on separately. As was the case with other Navy ships, the *Hunchback*'s black sailors were drawn largely from the ranks of ex-slaves: About twenty-five of the ship's roughly one hundred enlisted men were African American; fifteen were contrabands.

Scorched earth

William Tecumseh Sherman (above) was best known for the scorched-earth tactics of his "march to the sea," in which Union troops burned through the heart of the Confederate states. Charleston, South Carolina, where this group of black children sits amid the debris (left), was among the cities devastated by Sherman's troops. After the war, Sherman and Secretary of War Edwin M. Stanton invited African American ministers to Washington to discuss the future of the newly freed slaves. Four days later, Sherman issued a special order offering forty acres along the coast to ex-slave families.

Dignified images

These photographs were taken in the north by photographers who sought to depict black subjects with dignity and grace. The portrait of a black gentleman in formal attire has an elegant frame. The group of African American children, perhaps of mixed-race ancestry, was published in 1863 with the caption: "These children were turned out of the St Lawrence Hotel, Chestnut St., Philadelphia, on account of color." Another reference identifies them as slaves from New Orleans, where white masters sometimes acknowledged the children they had by slave women.

We look like men of war

Lincoln, concerned that it would prompt the border states to secede, initially rejected the deployment of black troops. So it was not until 1862 that volunteers, many of them ex-slaves, were placed under arms. All-black regiments were raised, like the 4th Colored Infantry (above), and by the end of the war nearly 180,000 black men had served as soldiers—about ten percent of enlistees.

Two

Years of Hope 1865–1877

A southern jury comprised of both blacks and whites, which could only have been constituted during the Reconstruction era.

Previous page
A southern school for freed slaves, 1870. For those who had been forbidden by law from learning to read, access to education was the sweetest harvest of freedom.

After the Civil War, Jourdon Anderson, a former slave from Tennessee then living in Dayton, Ohio, received a letter from his former master asking him to return to the plantation as a laborer. Anderson replied:

> Sir: I got your letter and was glad to find you had not forgotten Jourdon, and that you wanted me to come back and live with you again, promising to do better for me than anybody else can....
>
> As to my freedom, which you say I can have, there is nothing to be gained on that score, as I got my free-papers in 1864 from the Provost-Marshal-General of the Department of Nashville. Mandy says she would be afraid to go back without some proof that you are sincerely disposed to treat us justly and kindly—and we have concluded to test your sincerity by asking you to send us our wages for the time we served you. This will make us forget and forgive old scores, and rely on your justice and friendship in the future. I served you faithfully for thirty-two years and Mandy twenty years. At $25 a month for me, and $2 a week for Mandy, our earnings would amount to $11,680. Add to this the interest for the time our wages has been kept back and deduct what you paid for our clothing and three doctor's visits to me, and pulling a tooth for Mandy, and the balance will show what we are in justice entitled to. Please send the money by Adams Express, in care of V. Winters, esq., Dayton, Ohio. If you fail to pay us for faithful labors in the past we can have little faith in your promises in the future.
>
> In answering this letter please state if there would be any safety for my Milly and Jane, who are now grown up and both good-

looking girls. You know how it was with Matilda and Catherine. I would rather stay here and starve and die if it comes to that than have my girls brought to shame by the violence and wickedness of their young masters. You will also please state if there has been any schools opened for the colored children in your neighborhood, the great desire of my life now is to give my children an education, and have them form virtuous habits.

P. S. Say howdy to George Carter, and thank him for taking the pistol from you when you were shooting at me.
From your old servant,
Jourdon Anderson

An 1874 cartoon showing a member of the White League and a member of the Ku Klux Klan joining hands over a terrorized black family.

Jourdon Anderson's words crystallize the gains of the Reconstruction period: Schools were built, black leaders elected, and for the first time, African Americans had a measure of personal autonomy. Jourdan Anderson could write to his former master and demand back wages, an education for his children, and protection from the rape of black women by slave owners that was typical under slavery. His former owner might ask him to return. But Jourdon Anderson, now a free man, could refuse.

Anderson could reasonably expect his children to receive the education he hoped they would have. For those who had been forbidden by law from learning to read, access to education was the sweetest harvest of freedom. Between 1862, when the first "freedmen's" school was founded on St. Helena Island in South Carolina, and 1877, considered by most historians to be the end of Reconstruction, more than 600,000 African Americans had enrolled in thousands of schools established through the combined efforts of the federal government, northern abolitionists, and the ex-slaves themselves. Institutes of higher education were established as well: The Fisk Free Colored School, which would become Fisk University, in 1865, Howard University in 1866, and Hampton Normal and Agricultural Institute in 1868. These and other colleges founded in the Reconstruction period would be the mainstay of black higher education for generations to come.

An 1867 cartoon, "How Free Ballot Is Protected." White southerners both resented and feared the political power of African Americans after the war.

But African Americans remained vulnerable, particularly in the economic sphere. They were free, but they were also, as historian Lerone Bennett, Jr., put it, "free to the wind and to the rain, free to the wrath and hostility of their former slave masters. They had no tools, they had no shelter, they had no cooking utensils, and they were surrounded by hostile men who were determined to prove that the whole thing was a monstrous mistake."

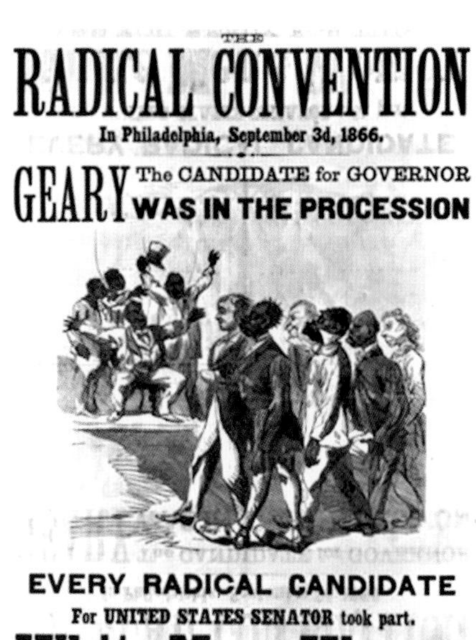

An 1866 poster attacking radical Republican politician John White Geary for his support of black suffrage.

An African American getting dressed beneath a picture of President Lincoln, 1868.

Despite African Americans' passionate appeals for a stake in the land they'd enriched for generations, and despite the federal promise of forty acres and a mule, post–Civil War governments failed to effectively redistribute land. As a result, though many freed people walked away from their former masters, others had no option but to continue the work they'd done as slaves—sometimes on the same plantations. In exchange for leasing small plots, black sharecroppers were to be paid when the crops came in—after deducting the planters' costs for housing, clothing, food, and supplies. In a system guaranteed to be exploitative, sharecroppers often ended the year deeper in debt than they began. In order to leave, sharecroppers had to first pay their debts, or face beatings and arrest.

Henry Blake of Little Rock, Arkansas, described the way sharecropping worked:

> After freedom…when we worked on shares, we couldn't make nothing—just overalls, and something to eat. Half went to the white man, and you would destroy your half, if you weren't careful. A man that didn't know how to count would always lose. He might lose anyhow. The white folks didn't give no itemized statements. No, you just had to owe so much. No matter how good account you kept, you had to go by their account, and now, brother, I'm telling you the truth about this—it's been that way for a long time. You had to take the white man's words and notes on everything. Anything you wanted you could get, if you were a good hand. If you didn't make no money, that's all right; they would advance you more. But you better not try to leave and get caught. They'd keep you in debt. They were sharp. Christmas come, you could take up twenty dollars in somethin'-to-eat and much as you wanted in whiskey. You could buy a gallon of whiskey—anything that kept you a slave. Because he was always right and you were always wrong, if there was a difference. If there was an argument, he would get mad and there would be a shooting take place.

The cotton industry, fueled by African Americans who were now sharecroppers rather than slaves, rebounded into renewed prosperity. The woman pictured on page 64, at work in a Georgia cotton field in 1870, likely did the same work she would have done as a slave.

The gains of Reconstruction were most significant in politics. Although African Americans did not win offices in proportion to their numbers, sixteen black elected officials served in Congress, over 600 in state legislatures, and hundreds more in local elected offices in the South during the Reconstruction years. In addition to adopting legislation aimed at improving the economic power of ex-slaves and making tax policies more equitable, Reconstruction governments established the South's first state-funded public schools. And though the relevant legislation generally went unenforced, Reconstruction governments barred racial discrimination in public transportation and accommodations.

A black preacher and his all-black congregation, 1876.

Those who had taken up arms to defend slavery never stopped trying to put political and economic control firmly back in the hands of white landowners and, by 1877, they succeeded. With an economic depression already dominating national attention, the infamous Tilden-Hayes compromise of that year gave the presidency to a northerner in exchange for the withdrawal of federal oversight in the South. In the words of historian Eric Foner, the former Confederates, now back in power, had put in place "a new racial system...resting on the disenfranchisement of black voters, a rigid system of racial segregation, the relegation of African Americans to low-wage agricultural and domestic employment, and legal and extralegal violence to punish those who challenged the new order." After Reconstruction, no African Americans would be elected to the U.S. Senate until the 1960s, and only two blacks would serve in the entire twentieth century. With its legacy of disenfranchisement of black voters, Mississippi, with a higher percentage of African Americans than any other state in the nation, would not send another black representative to Congress until 1986.

"The Freedmen's Bureau." An American officer separates white and black men.

Black Americans at the end of Reconstruction found themselves on their own. Frederick Douglass said in 1880, "The old master class is today triumphant, and the newly enfranchised class in a condition but little above that in which they were found before the rebellion."

Slaves to sharecroppers
A woman at work in a Georgia cotton field in 1870. After 1865 many of the newly free simply walked away from their former masters. Others had no option but to continue the work they'd done as slaves—sometimes on the same plantation. In the system that supplanted slavery, sharecroppers leased small plots and were to be paid at harvesttime—after deductions for housing, food, clothing, and supplies. Sharecroppers often ended the year deeper in debt than they began.

Slaves to shopkeepers
For some African Americans, the end of slavery did bring greater economic opportunity. Here, three shopkeepers, including one African American, stand in front of a grocery store in 1876. Their relative postures suggest the potential of new economic relations between blacks and whites during Reconstruction.

HAYES&REYNOLDS
PROVISIONS
WE SELL
FOR 4¢ PER

On the docks of New Orleans, 1870

For a time after the Civil War, African Americans held a majority of jobs on the New Orleans waterfront. Half of the better-paid longshoremen and yardmen were black, as were most lower-paid teamsters and railroad freight handlers. African American dockworkers even formed their own union, the Longshoremen's Protective Union Benevolent Association, in 1872. The Mississippi stern-wheeler riverboats seen here were vital to the growth of the cotton trade until the railroad network was built. Those on either side are passenger boats, but the one in the center is presumably waiting for its load of baled cotton to be transshipped to an oceangoing craft. The first steamship journey on the Mississippi was made in 1815. By 1830 there were 400 ships on it and the Ohio River. They were very prone to burst boilers—150 were recorded up to 1850, but in reality there were many more, often caused by rival captains racing each other. There were lurid stories of black crewmen being forced to sit on the safety valve to get those extra pounds of pressure.

King Cotton's Palace
A woman walks through ankle-high mounds of cotton at the Savannah Cotton Exchange, affectionately known by white Georgians as "King Cotton's Palace." Cotton exports had fallen after the Civil War, but by 1880, when this photo was taken, the local press estimated that "the cotton crop will net the producers and middlemen at least $2,750,000." Black workers like this woman did not share in the abundance.

The First African Church, Richmond
The largest of the African American churches in the Virginia capital, 1865. A year or two before, a white pastor preached "emphatically" against blacks enlisting in the Union Army. Black soldiers "abruptly left the building" and arrested him at the end of the service.

"Union of the races"
Thus was this mixed-race group on a porch in Jacksonville titled in a series of photographs, "Florida Views," from 1875. It speaks of an uneasy realignment as black emancipation, citizenship, and suffrage during Reconstruction brought a shift in race relations in the social sphere.

Congress and Senate

In 1862, Robert Smalls (above) was a slave crew member on the Confederate ship *The Planter.* One morning as his masters slept onshore, Smalls donned a Confederate Army cap and guided the vessel, with his family and other slaves onboard, safely to Union lines. He was elected to the U.S. Congress from South Carolina in 1875. Born a free man in North Carolina, Hiram Revels (right) served in the Union Army as a chaplain. In 1870, Revels was elected to fill the Mississippi seat in the U.S. Senate vacated by Jefferson Davis, who had been president of the Confederacy. He was the first African American to sit in the United States Senate.

Riverfront dock, Virginia African American maritime workers, even as slaves, had enjoyed greater freedom relative to those who worked on plantations; after emancipation, they were more economically stable, like this group of former slaves in 1865. Whether on the docks or onboard ships, black workers and seamen were in a unique position to receive and pass on critical information. They were key to shaping a new black identity after the Civil War.

Fisk University Jubilee Singers
The Fisk Jubilee Singers were organized in 1871 to raise money for the financially ailing Fisk Free Colored School, later to become Fisk University. The group's concert tours earned mass acclaim across the United States and Europe. For the Jubilee Singers' original members, most of whom were former slaves, the group's repertoire of African American spirituals had great meaning. Ella Shepard, a founding member, described the spirituals as songs "associated with slavery and the dark past," songs that were "sacred to our parents." They are photographed in Nashville, Tennessee, c. 1875.

The wrong side of the tracks?
Sitting on a railroad track on the outskirts of New Orleans, c. 1880 (above). In American towns the railroad often came to be the boundary between more affluent neighborhoods and those where poor whites and blacks lived. A family outside a tobacco-drying shed in Kentucky (right).

Thaddeus Stevens
This Republican Congressman attacked the moderate line taken toward the South by Lincoln and his successor Andrew Johnson at the end of the Civil War. Angry that the southern blacks were not getting a square deal, he and his fellow Republican Radicals forced through legislation for the right to vote. Stevens was chairman at the trial of Confederate President Andrew Jackson.

Convicts in chains
A gang, their legs chained together and in distinctive striped uniforms, unload mule carts at roadworks near Atlanta, Georgia, in the 1870s. They are beyond benefiting from the efforts of the Radicals. An armed white guard can be seen on the far sidewalk.

Buffalo Soldiers guarding a stagecoach, 1869

After the Civil War, the U.S. Army turned its attention to the conflicts raging with Native Americans. African Americans, including some former Union soldiers and ex-slaves, were attracted by the $13/month salary and the Army's promise to teach soldiers to read and write. Blacks were organized into segregated units and became known as Buffalo Soldiers.

Alone

A young African American man sits in front of a makeshift hut in the midst of a barren landscape. The era of Reconstruction ended in the later 1870s, leading to the disbanding of government protection for ex-slaves, suppression of the franchise, and institutionalized subordination. Frederick Douglass said in 1880, "The old master class is today triumphant, and the newly enfranchised class in a condition but little above that in which they were found before the rebellion."

Three

Self-Help or Retreat 1877–1900

Two new arrivals in Kansas, an "exoduster" and an Irishman, inspect each other.

W. E. B. Du Bois wrote of the post–Civil War era, "the slave went free; stood for a brief moment in the sun; then moved back again toward slavery." In the years following 1877, black farmers were driven off their land, black workers were paid unfair wages, black politicians were thrown out of office, and black voters were barred from the ballot box—all under the threat or reality of violence at the hands of the Ku Klux Klan and other white terror groups. It was not slavery. But by the turn of the century, the former plantocracy had erected a new framework for the economic and political subjugation of African Americans. White southerners called it "redemption," but for African Americans, the post-Reconstruction period would become known as a reign of terror. In the 1890s, lynch mobs claimed the lives of more African Americans than at any other time in American history.

In the late 1870s, Henry Adams of Louisiana concluded that African Americans had to leave the South to survive—even if it meant they had to desert the U.S. In a petition to President Rutherford B. Hayes, Adams asked that the besieged black population be given federal protection:

> If that protection cannot be given and our [Constitutional] rights [cannot be] restored, we would respectfully ask that some Territory be assigned to us in which we can colonize our race; and if that cannot be done, to appropriate means so that we can colonize in Liberia or some other country, for we feel and know that unless full and ample protection is guaranteed to us, we cannot live in the South, and will and must colonize under some other government, and we put our full trust in God that our prayers and petition will be speedily answered.

Previous page
An ex-slave family of homesteaders poses outside their Nebraska sod house, 1888. With the growing repression and economic hardship at the end of Reconstruction, thousands fled the South in search of freedom and opportunity. In what came to be known as the "Black Exodus," freed people resettled in Oklahoma, Nebraska, Indiana, and, particularly, Kansas.

Benjamin "Pap" Singleton helped organize a large contingent of African Americans to leave the South for Kansas and other points west. When asked to defend his actions before a U.S. Senate committee investigating the black exodus, Singleton proudly answered, "Yes, sir; I am the whole cause of the Kansas immigration! I think I have done a good deal of good, and I feel relieved!"

The federal government, which had already turned a deaf ear to black concerns, ignored the petition and allowed harassment and intimidation of southern African Americans to continue. But Adams and tens of thousands of others took action: They left. In southern black communities, pamphlets and posters were printed, meetings and debates were held, and plans were drawn up. By the spring of 1879, the banks of the Mississippi heaved with hundreds of black families and all their possessions, clamoring to board steamships that would take them north to St. Louis, where they would make their way to Kansas—the "Negro Canaan."

Altogether, nearly 15,000 African Americans fled the south for Kansas in 1879 and 1880; thousands more sought refuge, land, and freedom in Nebraska and other western territories. They defied the southern landowners who, bemoaning the loss of their labor, tried to prevent their departure. The movement west drew criticism from Frederick Douglass, who argued that blacks should stand their ground in the South. But the "exodusters" persevered and those who headed west made their own way. Although they continued to face economic hardship, they enjoyed greater autonomy. About three-quarters came to own homes, their children were more likely than not to attend school (girls at a higher rate than boys), and illiteracy among the westward migrants was less than ten percent.

Whether they stayed in the South or migrated north or west, with the withdrawal of federal support, African Americans found themselves increasingly alone when it came to developing institutions to address the legacy of slavery. African Americans almost completely withdrew from white-controlled religious organizations to form independent churches. At the same time, there was a flowering of black fraternal, benevolent, and mutual benefit societies.

And even in these difficult years, African Americans kept their focus on education. They drew on the support of northern philanthropists and a measure of state financing, but black schools were established, teachers trained, and schoolhouses built largely with the sweat of black brows. An unprecedented number of African Americans were educated at the primary level and in institutions of higher learning. And while only a fraction of the black population could read at the close of the Civil War, by the turn of the twentieth century, illiteracy among African Americans was all but eliminated. African American women, such as Mary Church Terrell, were key leaders in the struggle for education.

Benjamin Tucker Tanner (1835–1923) was the eighteenth bishop of the African Methodist Episcopal Church and author of *An Apology for African Methodism*, a treatise addressing the history of the church and criticism of it by outsiders. He was the father of painter Henry Ossawa Tanner. The A.M.E. Church was known for its philanthropic and self-help activities.

In the political arena, by far the most significant event of the post-Reconstruction period was the emergence of Booker T. Washington and a new generation of black leadership. Washington founded Tuskegee Institute in Alabama in 1881, with a program of both academic and vocational training. Under his leadership, Tuskegee became a national model for black self-improvement through industry and manual labor, and Washington himself became a prominent, if ultimately controversial, spokesperson. Rather than destabilize race relations by pressing demands for social and political equality, Washington argued, African Americans should strive for economic stability while tolerating social subordination. In a major speech at the 1895 Cotton Exhibition in Atlanta, Georgia, Washington outlined his program for black progress. "In all things that are purely social," he said, "we can be as separate as the fingers, yet one as the hand in all things essential to mutual progress."

His program of accommodation to racial subordination would soon be subject to withering criticism from more radical African American leaders, including W. E. B. Du Bois and Ida B. Wells-Barnett. But in the years before the turn of the twentieth century, Booker T. Washington was by far the most prominent and influential black leader in the United States.

Washington's stance could not have come at a more critical time. In 1890, the post-Reconstruction governor of Louisiana signed a law segregating that state's railways. The law mandated that trains provide "equal but separate" cars for blacks and whites, and prohibited individuals of different races from riding together or face twenty-five-dollar fine or twenty days in jail.

The new law stirred opposition among African Americans in New Orleans, but when a columnist for a black-owned newspaper suggested a boycott, Washington preached patience and accommodation. Washington's influence and black fears of violent reprisals stifled the protest.

Two years later, thirty-year-old black shoemaker Homer Plessy refused to leave his seat on a New Orleans train. His action would start a series of legal cases ending in the 1896 U.S. Supreme Court decision legalizing segregation According to the majority opinion, the object of the 13th Amendment to the Constitution, which abolished slavery, "could not have been intended to abolish distinctions based upon color," and that laws requiring the separation of the races "do not imply the inferiority of either race to the other." In a single stroke, the Supreme Court legitimized the notion that schools and public accommodations could be required to be "separate but equal."

Justice John Marshall Harlan, a southerner, cast the one vote in support of Homer Plessy and wrote a lone but powerful dissent. Legal segregation, Harlan wrote, allowed "the seeds of race hate to be planted under the sanctions of law…the thin disguise of 'equal' accommodations…will not mislead anyone, nor atone for the wrong this day done."

The legal segregation sanctioned by *Plessy v. Ferguson* would stand until a series of cases beginning with *Brown v. Board of Education* in 1954, more than sixty years later.

A railroad advertisement shows a Pullman car attendant serving two passengers.

Still on the plantation
The nature of work on this cotton plantation in 1895 has changed little since the days of slavery, but these African Americans—women, men, and children—are free, even though they must continue to fill the bushel baskets.

Self-respect
African American women who left the South may have gained greater control over their lives. A woman nursing an infant outside her home appears to be very much at ease, as an older child smiles on the porch, 1894.

Cleaning cotton
Instead of babies on their knees, these women have piles of cotton, which they are preparing for the mill in the 1880s. Their workday dress has not altered since the days of slavery.

At the French Market, New Orleans
Children in the streets of the French Quarter of New Orleans in 1890. The same year, a race riot, with rampant violence by whites against blacks, swept through the city. From the stance of his legs, the boy on the left might well be suffering from rickets, caused by vitamin D deficiency.

Black cowboys
About twenty-five percent of the cowboys who drove herds of cattle over hundreds of miles of rough and dangerous terrain from Texas to the cattle markets up north were African American. These black cowboys are outside Bonham, Texas, 1885.

Out West
White and McMahon's drugstore and soda fountain in Denver, Colorado, sometime before 1900, serving African American women, who are as fancily dressed as their white companion.

Cane and cotton
Four boys, two holding sugarcane, stand before bales of raw cotton in Aiken, South Carolina, in the 1890s. Most African Americans lived in former Confederate states; most, including children, were still engaged in agricultural labor.

Making music
A boy sits by the door of a hand-hewn log house playing a homemade stringed instrument in the 1890s, perhaps soothing the pain from his injured toe.

Cotton cars
These are loaded for transportation north from Atlanta, Georgia, c. 1880. Atlanta hosted the International Cotton Exhibition in 1882. One account of the exhibition summarized its economic importance while making no mention of the black laborers on whom the industry depended: "Receipts were from $220,000 to $250,000.... The amount of sales made of improved machinery was simply marvelous."

Construction work
African American workers dig a sewer down a street in Savannah, Georgia, c. 1890. The two well-dressed men standing at left appear to be playing the role of overseers. The containers on the crossbeam hold food and drinks.

MUSIC

Contrasts in schooling

Education, wherever it was enjoyed, was the sweetest harvest of freedom.
A tiny wooden schoolhouse in Savannah, Georgia (left), c. 1890. The bespectacled and top-hatted figure is the teacher, and the pile of wood is fuel for his fire. An integrated class, including four African American children (above), c. 1900.

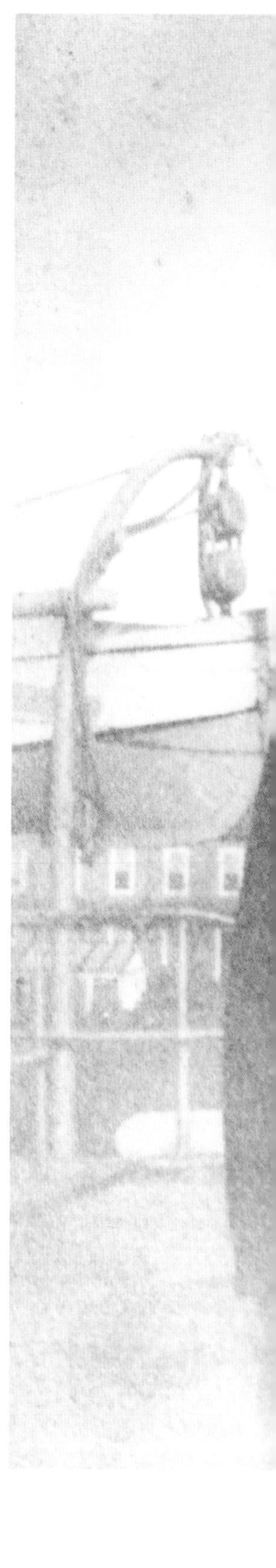

Inside and outside the system

The expression and body language of this Louisiana boy convey humor and confidence (left). Boys who scavenged a living on the riverside were called "levee rats." Two members of the crew of the U.S.S. *Newark* in 1898, part of the Navy that was to defeat the Spanish in Cuba and the Philippines that year (right).

Exhibitions

The famous Paris "Exposition Universelle" in 1900 included an "Exhibit of American Negroes" curated by W. E. B. Du Bois, which featured photos of important African American buildings: the Metropolitan African Methodist Church (next page, bottom right) and St. Augustine's Catholic Church (next page, bottom left), both in Washington, D.C. The premises of "The Bee" (top left) were there also, while the Coleman Manufacturing Company's factory, the only African American cotton mill in the U.S., was in Concord, North Carolina (bottom left) and an African American–owned shop (bottom right) was in Chicago. Another photograph shown at Paris was this group of African American Roman Catholic Nuns, Sisters of the Holy Family, from New Orleans (next page, top). Next to them is a view of the "Flags of Freedom" Negro Building (top right) at the Atlanta Expo, Georgia, 1896, an important showcase for the cotton industry.

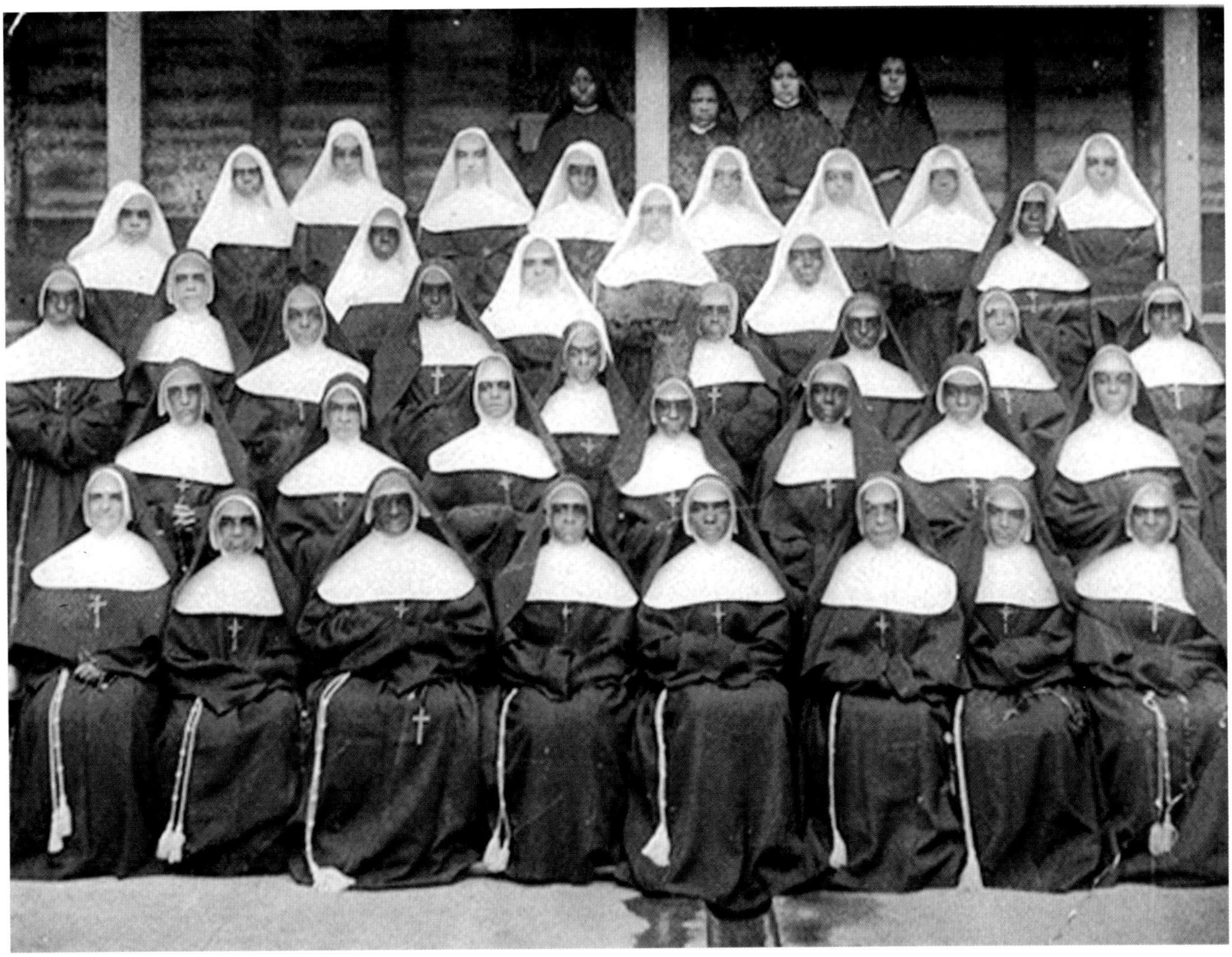

Cakewalk

Movements derived from slave dances—and in some cases African dance—became all the rage in European and American ballrooms around the turn of the century. The cakewalk, performed here at the PanAm Expo in Buffalo, New York, was influenced by the African American "ring shout."

George Washington Carver
As head of the agriculture department at Tuskegee Institute, botanist (and former slave) George Washington Carver devised innovative crop rotation methods and developed over three hundred peanut products. In 1916, Carver would be appointed to The Royal Society of Arts in London, England.

Students at work
A laboratory at Tuskegee Institute in Alabama. Founded in 1881, Tuskegee was led by Booker T. Washington until his death in 1915. Washington, who urged African Americans to strive for economic independence rather than social and political equality, would become the most prominent black leader of the late nineteenth century.

Serious musicians

A group of young musicians from Georgia, two of them mandolin players. This photograph is from an album compiled by W. E. B. Du Bois, c. 1900.

Higher learning

The main building of Howard University in Washington, D.C. Founded in 1867, it was transformed into a major institution in the 1920s by its first black president, Mordecai Johnson. Booker T. Washington (right, center), appointed to the university's board of trustees in 1907, is photographed the year before at the twenty-fifth anniversary of the Tuskegee Institute, of which he was founding president. With him are some of the philanthropists who helped found it, including Andrew Carnegie (bottom row, second from right).

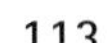

Four

The Great Migration and World War I 1900–1920

Afro-Americans of Augusta, Ga., are boycotting the street cars of that city because they have been compelled to ride in the back seats. This is carrying the "Jim Crow" business to street cars—"rubbing it in," as it were. Our people form such a large portion of the population of Augusta that they have only to keep up the boycott they have so wisely instituted to so affect the financial condition of the street car company as to convince them in the best way possible of the contemptibleness of their latest "color line." We sincerely trust that not an Afro-American in Augusta, will ride on a car when they can possibly help it as long as the "Jim Crow" color line exists.

Boycotting Jim Crow: report in the *Cleveland Gazette* of September 1898.

The January 6, 1917, headline of the African American newspaper *The Chicago Defender* trumpeted, "Millions to Leave South." Inside the paper, publisher Robert Sengstacke Abbott printed editorials, cartoons, poems, and letters in a campaign to urge the *Defender*'s southern readers to come north. The paper even printed one-way train schedules from southern stations to Chicago.

Southern African Americans had plenty of reasons to respond to Abbott's seductive descriptions of the good life in the north. Beginning in 1913, black agricultural workers already on the economic margins were made even more vulnerable by a depression in the cotton market, a devastating infestation of boll weevils, and severe floods that ruined countless southern homes and farms.

The southern economy was reeling, but in the North, as the United States prepared to enter World War I in 1917, the number of relatively well-paying industrial jobs exploded. Steel mills, packing houses, automobile plants, and construction projects opened up to African Americans for the first time. Between 1916 and 1919, half a million African Americans in search of prosperity and freedom poured out of the South; in the 1920s, a million more followed them.

Previous page
"A bunch of Chicago boys," 1917.
Black troops served eagerly and valiantly in World War I.

In the North and the new cities of the West, the migrants found not only better wages, but the freedom to vote, less racial violence, and, sometimes, better schools. But Chicago and New York were hardly the Promised Land. Discrimination in housing, jobs, and education was real and thorough. Black men were often relegated to menial assignments; black women, though some found factory work, more often had to work as domestics. And African Americans were largely excluded from the labor unions that might have offered job security and protection from workplace abuses.

Among the migrants were musicians who carried with them African Americans' rich artistic traditions. Jazz had emerged in New Orleans around the turn of the century, but beginning with the Great Migration this new and vibrant music captured the attention of the world. Marching bands such as the Excelsior Brass Band, the Olympia Brass Band, and the original Tuxedo Band helped diffuse New Orleans–style jazz. Jelly Roll Morton left New Orleans to travel with vaudeville troupes around the country before settling in Chicago in 1910. Other musicians who were influential in the development of jazz migrated north as well: King Oliver and Sidney Bechet to Chicago and then New York; Kid Ory to California; and in 1922 Louis Armstrong left New Orleans for Chicago and, two years later, New York City. Through touring, recording, and popular radio performances, these and other black musicians who originated in the South redefined American popular culture.

Jim Crow Law Upheld.

Washington—The "Jim Crow" law of Kentucky, reqiuring different coaches for whites and colored, was upheld today by the supreme court. The South Covington and Cincinnati Street Railway Co. brought a test of the law before the supreme court in an appeal to set aside fines for its violations which has been sustained in the lower courts. The decisions of the lower court were affirmed.

Justices Day, Vandevanter and Pitney dissented from the opinion of the court.

Report in the *Ohio State Monitor*, April 1920.

African Americans became more visible in Hollywood, though they were largely restricted to stereotypical roles and images. D. W. Griffith's 1915 film *Birth of a Nation,* a box office hit that was hailed as a cinematic breakthrough, romanticized slavery and cast the Ku Klux Klan as heroes. Whites like Al Jolson drew on the minstrel tradition, performing "blackface" caricatures of African Americans. Black performers who did come to prominence had to put their prodigious talents in the service of strictly proscribed roles. African Americans had little power to shape the images projected of them in popular culture. But there were a handful of African American filmmakers in the 1910s and '20s, most notably Oscar Micheaux, who drew black characters and black life on a broader canvas.

A stereotypical happy black cook, with a watermelon grin and a bad command of English, helps sell ham in the 1920s. The Chicago stockyards, from which the Armour meat products came, employed thousands of the blacks who migrated from the South.

The Great Migration already under way, America's entry into World War I in 1917 further heightened black expectations for progress. Among black leaders, participation in the war effort was debated: Was this a "white man's war" in which an oppressed minority had no interest, or an opportunity to prove blacks' courage and patriotism, and thus worthiness of full citizenship? W. E. B. Du Bois called on African Americans to "close our ranks shoulder to shoulder with our white fellow citizens." Unstinting patriotism, he wrote, would result in "the right to vote and the right to work and the right to live without insult."

Women from Guadeloupe, West Indies, upon their arrival at Ellis Island, New York, onboard the SS *Korona*, 1911. Caribbean immigrants were among those who flocked to the United States in the early decades of the twentieth century.

Black leaders overcame stubborn resistance in order to have African Americans included in the wartime draft. Ultimately, nearly 370,000 black men were drafted—all into strictly segregated units under the command of white officers. Two hundred thousand black soldiers were deployed to Europe, some forty thousand of whom saw combat.

Because American military leaders were reluctant to put black troops into the field, many were turned over to French army command. Black troops experienced greater social acceptance and more equal treatment from the French than from the U.S. Army. In the 369th Regiment, popularly known as the Harlem Hellfighters, an astonishing 171 African Americans received military honors from the French government. In contrast, no black soldier who served in World War I received the Congressional Medal of Honor, America's highest award for military heroism, until President George Bush presented relatives of Cpl. Freddie Stowers with what he termed a "long overdue" Medal of Honor in 1991.

Ida B. Wells-Barnett (1862–1931) was a pioneering journalist and a leader in the movements for civil and women's rights. In 1892, after the brutal murder of three black businessmen, Wells wrote a series of blistering editorials in her newspaper, the *Memphis Free Speech*. The newspaper's office was burned down in retaliation. But Wells continued to write and lecture, traveling throughout the United States and Europe to garner support for an antilynching law. With Frederick Douglass, she wrote a pamphlet critical of African Americans' absence from the 1893 World's Fair; in 1910 she was among the founders of the NAACP.

On the home front, Du Bois's hopes that proof of black patriotism would lead to social progress were dashed. Competition over jobs and white hostility toward the influx of black migrants brought racial tensions in many urban areas to the boiling point. In July 1917, just months after America's entry into World War I, rumors that a black man had shot a white storekeeper ripped through East St. Louis. In response, local whites exploded in the worst racial rioting the country had ever seen. Black homes, churches, and businesses were set afire. Carloads of whites drove through black neighborhoods, shooting at drivers and pedestrians indiscriminately as the police stood by. By the time the violence came under control, thirty-nine whites and more than a hundred African Americans had been killed.

East St. Louis was only the beginning. In what became known as the Red Summer of 1919, race riots erupted in more than two dozen cities from Washington, D.C., to Omaha, Nebraska, as resentful whites vented their wrath against black economic and social progress. Among the worst of the 1919 riots occurred in Chicago, where twenty-three African Americans and fifteen whites died, hundreds more were injured, and the National Guard was mobilized to quell the violence.

The race riots of 1917–1919, the accelerated pace of lynchings—sometimes of black soldiers in uniform—and the resurgence of the Ku Klux Klan inspired a more militant style of black leadership. W. E. B.

Du Bois, Ida B. Wells, and others were deeply opposed to Booker T. Washington's message of accommodation to second-class status. Instead, they demanded that black American citizens be granted the same civil rights enjoyed by whites. The NAACP, founded in 1909, and its short-lived predecessor, the Niagara Movement, had the stated goal of securing the rights guaranteed in the 13th, 14th, and 15th Amendments to the United States Constitution, which promised an end to slavery, the equal protection of the law, and universal adult male suffrage. The NAACP established its national office in New York City and named Moorfield Storey, a white constitutional lawyer, president. By 1913, the NAACP had established branch offices in Boston, Kansas City, Washington, D.C., Detroit, and St. Louis, and Du Bois, the only African American among the organization's founding executives, was a well-regarded spokesman and editor of *The Crisis*, the official journal of the NAACP.

Marcus Garvey (1887–1940), the founder of the Universal Negro Improvement Association (UNIA). He arrived penniless in New York from Jamaica in 1916 and within three years had built the largest black organization in history.

The NAACP was not the only expression of growing black discontent and impatience. An even more militant political stance was taken by Marcus Garvey, a Jamaican-born nationalist leader. Rather than calling for integration, Garvey's program urged the creation of independent black institutions. By 1919, with a combination of fiery oratory, pan-Africanist philosophy, and business development, Garvey had built his Universal Negro Improvement Association into the largest black organization in American history.

The Great Migration and World War I set the stage for the emergence of a self-assured, sophisticated, and politically militant black leadership, and the flowering of African American culture known as the Harlem Renaissance.

Cutting cane
A boy learning how to cut sugarcane as a white man looks on, Louisiana, 1900. Working conditions for most African Americans remained unchanged in the South.

In Manhattan

A group of African American workers stand with pickaxes and shovels, removing the foundation of the old Plaza Hotel in preparation for the construction of the present Plaza Hotel, at Fifth Avenue and Fifty-ninth Street, c. 1905. The Plaza is a recognized landmark at the southern end of Central Park.

A sewing class

William J. Edwards, a Tuskegee graduate and protégé of Booker T. Washington, started the Snow Hill Normal and Industrial School in 1893 with a fifty-cent endowment, three students, and a log cabin. Snow Hill envolved into an acclaimed academic and vocational school.

The Niagara Movement

The founding members of this forerunner of the National Association for the Advancement of Colored People (NAACP), with the falls behind them. W. E. B. Du Bois is second from the right in the middle row.

Jazz roots

An all-saxophone novelty group, c. 1900, snappily dressed in top hats, frock coats, and spats, with a picture hat and tailored outfit for the woman. The saxophone came into its own fifteen or twenty years after this picture, thanks largely to Sidney Bechet.

The original Tuxedo Band

The New Orleans–based group, seen here in 1917, toured the southern Gulf states and went on to make a number of recordings in the 1920s. Many of its members later became prominent jazz musicians. Bandleader Oscar "Papa" Celestin is third from the left in the back row.

Louis Armstrong

Louis "Satchmo" Armstrong at the age of twelve, with other members of the Waif's Home Colored Brass Band, New Orleans, Louisiana, 1913. Armstrong is third from left in the second row. He would rise to become one of the most influential musicians of the twentieth century. "Satchmo" was short for "Satchelmouth." Thanks to his unique abilities as a trumpet player and as an entertainer, he became one of the most influential musicians ever, in particular moving jazz on from the jerky rhythms of ragtime to a smoother swing.

Jelly Roll Morton

This pioneering American jazz pianist and composer (third from left) with musicians (left to right) "Common Sense" Ross, Albertine Pickens, Ada "Bricktop" Smith, Eddie Rucker, and Mabel Watts, is outside the Cadillac Café in Los Angeles, California, 1917. At age twelve, Morton began his musical career playing piano in the rough Storyville district of New Orleans. In the 1920s he recorded some of his most famous compositions with his group, the Red Hot Peppers: "Kansas City Stomp" and "Smokehouse Blues." Clarinetist Johnny Dods and trombonist Kid Ory were both members of the Peppers.

Wild West

Prominent rodeo rider Jess Stahl atop his bucking horse Crow Foot at the Harney County Roundup, Burns, Oregon, 1928 (above). Isom Dart (1855–1900), a black rustler originally known as Ned Huddleston, Denver, Colorado (right). Dart was shot and killed by a bounty hunter in Brown's Park, Colorado.

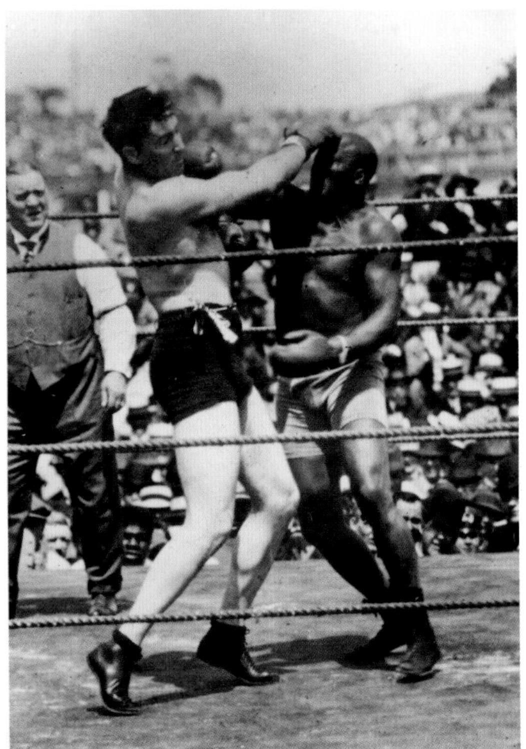

Jack Johnson

When boxer Jack Johnson captured the heavyweight title in 1908, he became a hero among black Americans. But his success, and his public courting of white women, enraged many whites. Johnson's easy defeat of former champion Jim Jeffries, the "Great White Hope," in 1910 sparked white riots in several cities, and six African Americans were killed in New York City alone. Johnson held the heavyweight title until 1915, when he was defeated by Jess Willard, a white Kansan, in Havana, Cuba (left). He poses in a racing car, in 1911 (above).

Matthew Henson

On April 6, 1909, Matthew Henson (right) planted the American flag at the North Pole, as part of an expedition led by Commander Robert E. Peary. Originally hired by Peary as a valet, he became indispensable to him on seven polar expeditions because of his navigational skills and because he could speak Inuit.

Chalmers
"30"

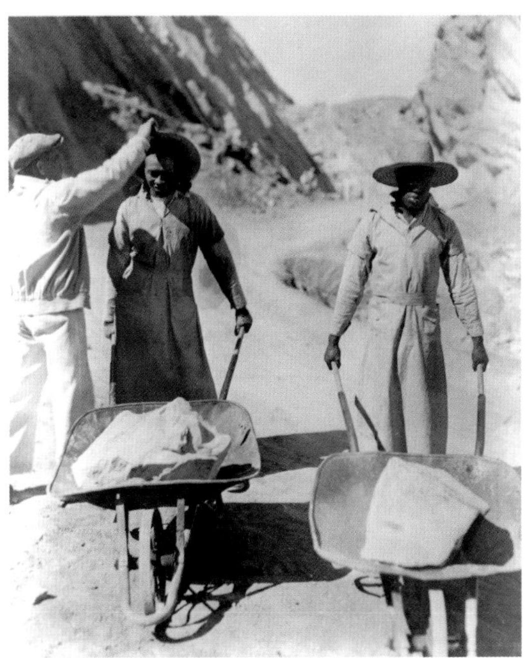

Convict life

Black prisoners in straw hats and dresses at the Colorado State Penitentiary, Canon City, in the 1900s. Their outfits and their task, wheeling lumps of rock, seem to be special punishments intended to humiliate them (above). A gang making a road at Little Rock, Arkansas, c. 1910 (left), while the occupants of a Chalmers 30 automobile look on. The scene is little changed from that on p. 79.

Execution

A condemned African American is led into the execution chamber on the arm of a chaplain at the notorious Sing Sing prison, Ossining, New York (above), before being strapped into the electric chair (right), c. 1900.

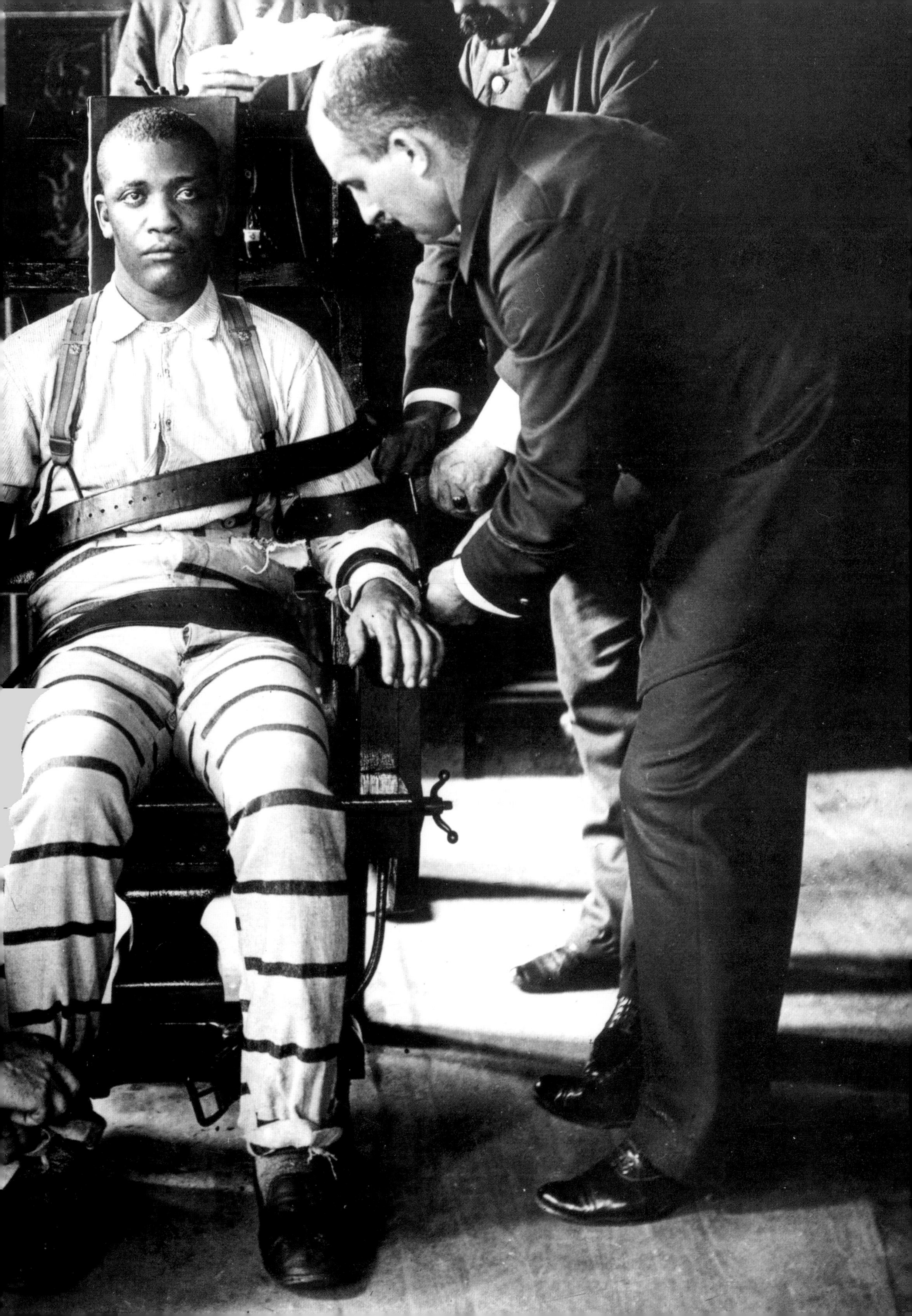

Looking for work

Boys and men, black and white, outside a labor agency in New York, 1912. Jobs in track-work and freight-handling on the Erie Railroad, Buffalo Division, are advertised, the latter paying $2.40 a day. Construction work pays $3 a day. Other jobs in coal mining in West Virginia and in iron mining are also advertised.

ONAL
GENCY 355
SHIP
EVERY
DAY
For
Construction
2 75
Per Day
STO
TO
A.A.SO
53-35
• TEL.OR
POST NO
50 MEN
COAL MINES

Small business
The proprietor of a watchmaking and jewelry business stands proudly at his shop door in Richmond, Virginia, during the 1900s.

Big business

Madame C. J. Walker takes the wheel in 1911. Selling hair-care products and cosmetics through a network of agents and advertisements in the black press, Walker became the country's first self-made woman millionaire. In 1917 she helped lead a protest against lynching and donated heavily to the NAACP. After her death in 1919, her daughter A'lelia kept a literary salon during the Harlem Renaissance.

Scavenging and sharpening

Boys collect scrap timber for firewood, 1910 (above), their "soap-box" carts equipped with recycled baby carriage wheels. Children watching a saw-sharpener at work on Seventh Avenue, near Thirtieth Street, New York, 1904 (right).

ABE. WEINBERG
2437
CLASS
&
PICTURE FRAMES
SILVERERS OF
NEW & OLD MIRRORS
PICTURE
FRAMES
TO
ORDER

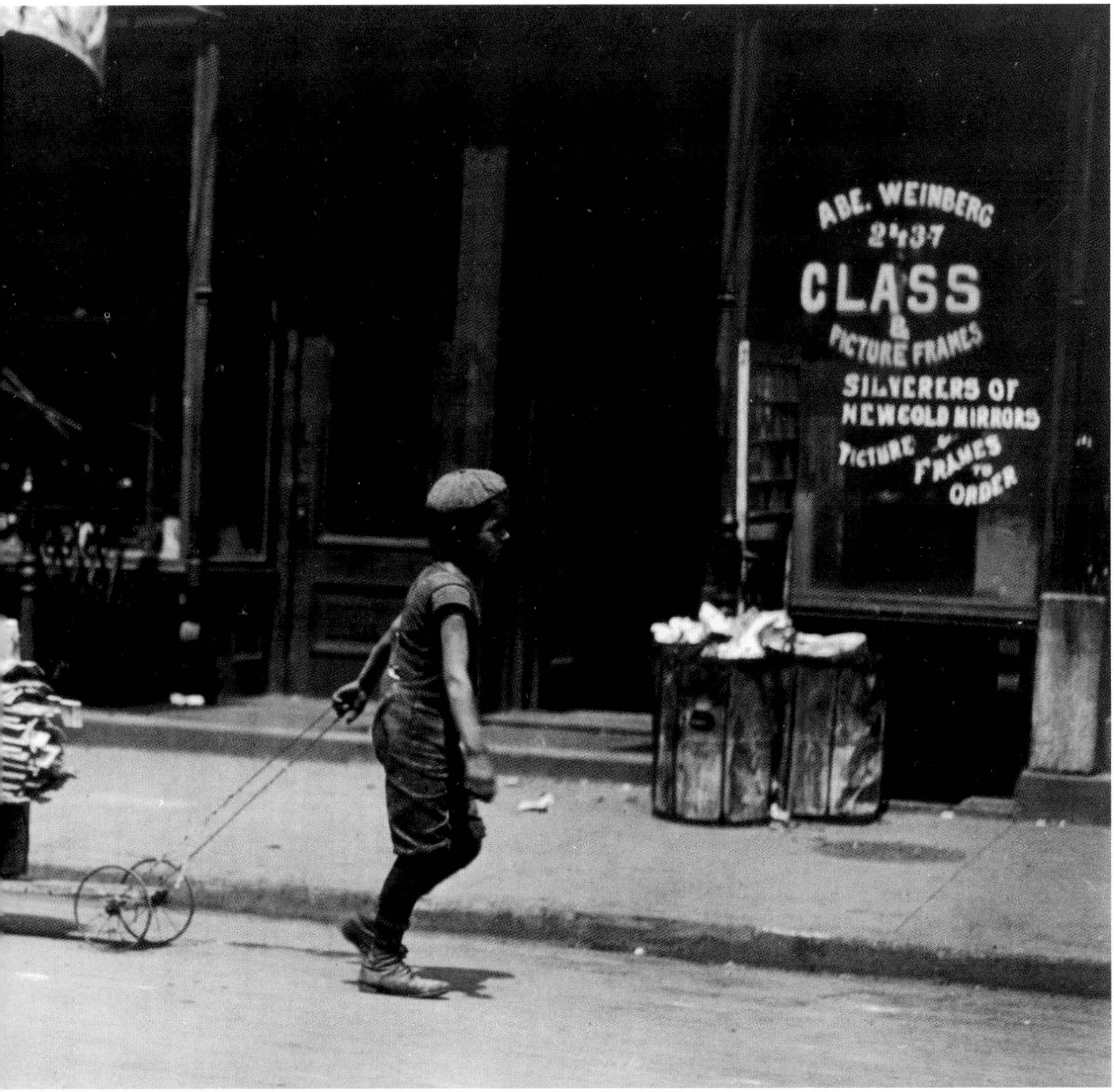

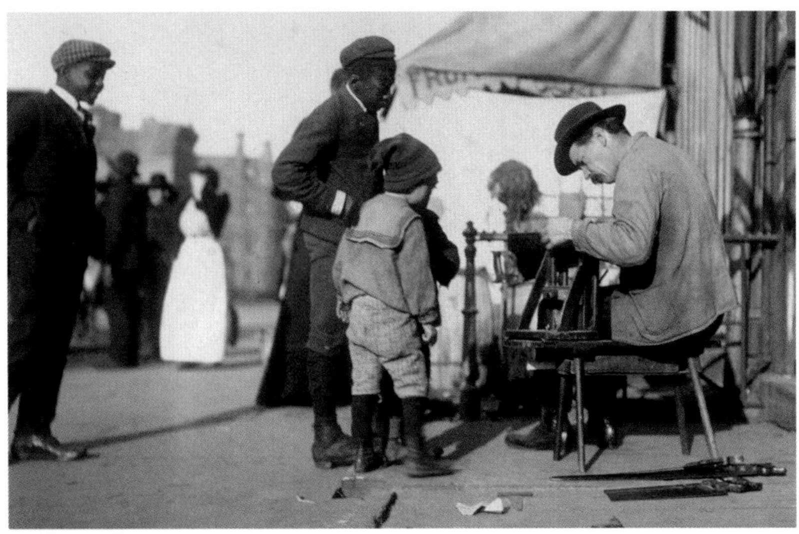

Out and about

Black and white children aboard a carousel at Coney Island, New York (right). In its early years, Coney Island was a seaside haven for the less privileged of the city. As with other American amusement parks, days were set aside specifically for black customers to avoid alienating white customers with mixed crowds. This carefully contrived photograph could have been intended to promote interracial attendance or been taken by an open-minded community organization, but it is unlikely to have been taken by chance. A uniformed nursemaid and her two well-dressed charges in Washington, D.C., 1910 (above). She probably would have preferred to have been photographed on her day off and in her own clothes.

First World War
African American soldiers going to the front (above). A German officer with a prisoner from a Harlem regiment (right), and other Allied prisoners-of-war behind.

In the line and out
African American troops man a trench alongside French Colonial troops (above). Wounded soldiers line up for Red Cross chocolate and sandwiches in Toulouse (left). Many African Americans were under French command because the U.S. military were reluctant to use them. The French, on the other hand, had used Senegalese and other colonial troops for many years.

Back home

Henry Johnson receives a hero's welcome in the U.S. He was one of the first two Americans—both black—to be awarded the Croix de Guerre by France (above). The "famous 15th New York Regiment," which went away singing, now returns from France, still singing (right). Two hundred thousand black soldiers were deployed there and forty thousand saw combat.

THOU
SHALT
NOT
KILL

Red Summer

In what became known as the Red Summer of 1919, race riots erupted across the country. In more than two dozen cities, from Washington, D.C., to Omaha, Nebraska, resentful whites vented their wrath against black economic and social progress. One of the deadliest of the riots occurred in Chicago, where twenty-three African Americans and fifteen whites died and hundreds more were injured. The National Guard (above) was called on to quell the violence.

March against lynching

The NAACP, led by W. E. B. Du Bois, sponsored a silent march of ten thousand up New York's Fifth Avenue in July 1917 to protest rising antiblack violence—particularly the East St. Louis riot in which between forty and two hundred were killed. Black boy scouts distributed leaflets explaining "We march because we deem it a crime to be silent in the face of such barbaric acts." Many African American leaders believed, like Du Bois, that unswerving black patriotism in the war would be rewarded with "the right to vote and the right to work and the right to live without insult." But racial violence, including the lynching of some African Americans in uniform, continued during the war.

The Tulsa riot

Injured and wounded are being taken to the hospital by National Guardsmen, June 3, 1921, after the race riots. The prosperous black Tulsa, Oklahoma, community of Greenwood was known as the "Negro Wall Street of America." But whites were resentful of black success, and in May 1921, allegations that a black man had assaulted a white woman touched off a riot. Armed whites descended on Greenwood, burning houses, firebombing businesses, and shooting residents at random. Though African Americans fought back, they were badly outgunned; hundreds died on both sides. Over one thousand black houses and businesses were burned (above). Government action compounded Greenwood's injuries: Six thousand people, approximately half of Tulsa's black population, were reportedly incarcerated during the riot; then, when promised reconstruction of their homes faltered, a thousand black Tulsans spent the winter in tents.

Ku Klux Klan
Members of the terrorist white supremacist organization crawling out of a tunnel after a meeting, November 1922.

The Klan in the nation's capital

Forty thousand members of the Ku Klux Klan parade down Washington's Pennsylvania Avenue in 1925. A measure of the Klan's comfort in the nation's capital is indicated by members marching with their trademark hoods and robes—but without masks covering their faces. The year before, the KKK had claimed 4.5 million members.

ICE COLD
Jax
ALE
STOUT
PRINCE
ALBERT
COLORED
ONLY
POLICE
ORDER
ROYAL CROWN

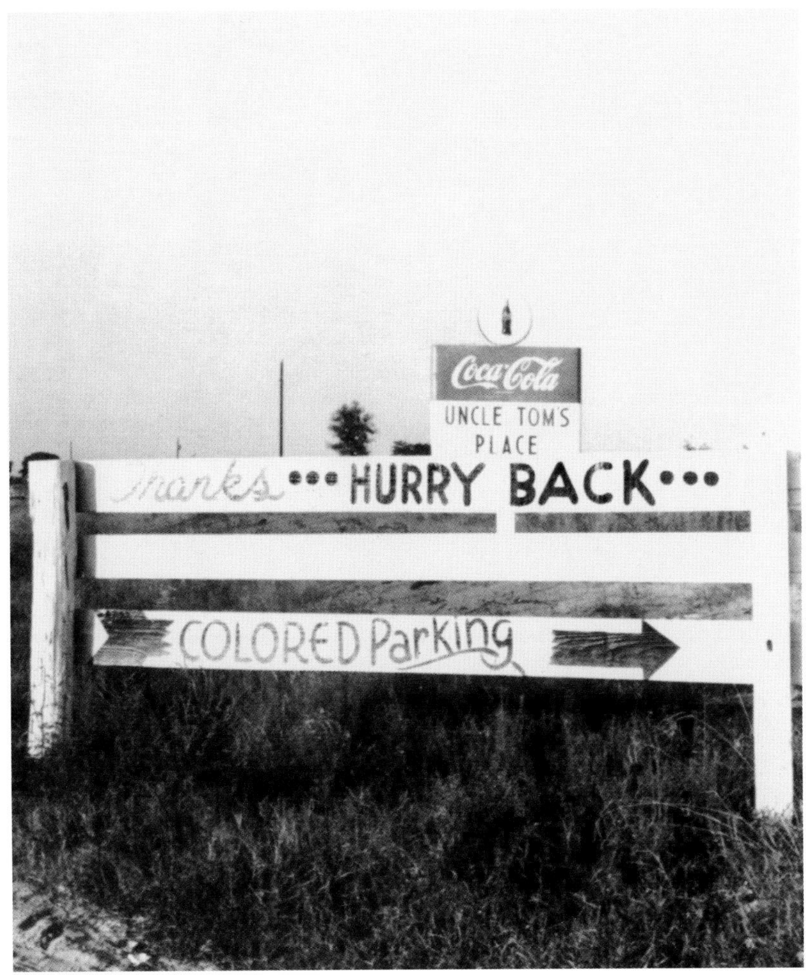

Segregated shopping

The signs say it all. A "colored only" store, so designated by "police order," somewhere in the South, c. 1925 (left). White-owned businesses, such as "Uncle Tom's Place" (above), went to extremes to keep the races separate in all respects—entrances, toilets, even parking—in spite of often being dependent on black customers.

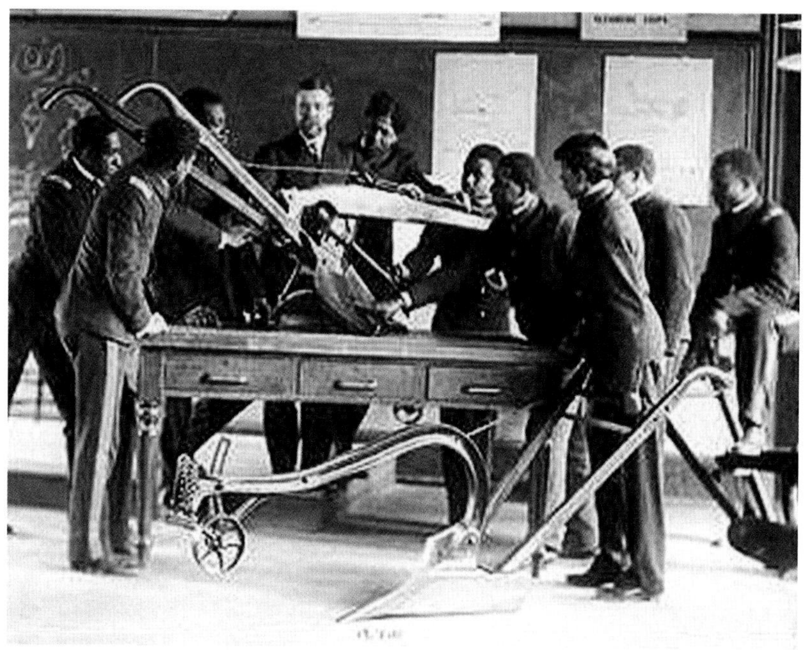

An urge to learn

African Americans continued to flock to educational opportunities wherever they existed. Uniformed students of Hampton Institute receive instruction about plows, c. 1900 (above). Adults learning to read and write in a southern classroom, 1920 (right).

My man is new
We were new men
Many men are in Rome
No man is new
No one is near
I win a pony
My boy won a pony
I am a woman
Men marry women
I wipe my pen
Buy me a pen
You may pay me
Please pay me now
Our money is our pay
Pay your money now

Higher education

The "Class of '17" at Howard University in Washington, D.C. (above). Members of the Morris Brown College baseball team, c. 1900 (right), attended one of several colleges founded and supported by black religious organizations. The college was named in honor of a bishop of the African Methodist Episcopal (AME) Church, Atlanta, Georgia.

MORRIS
BROWN

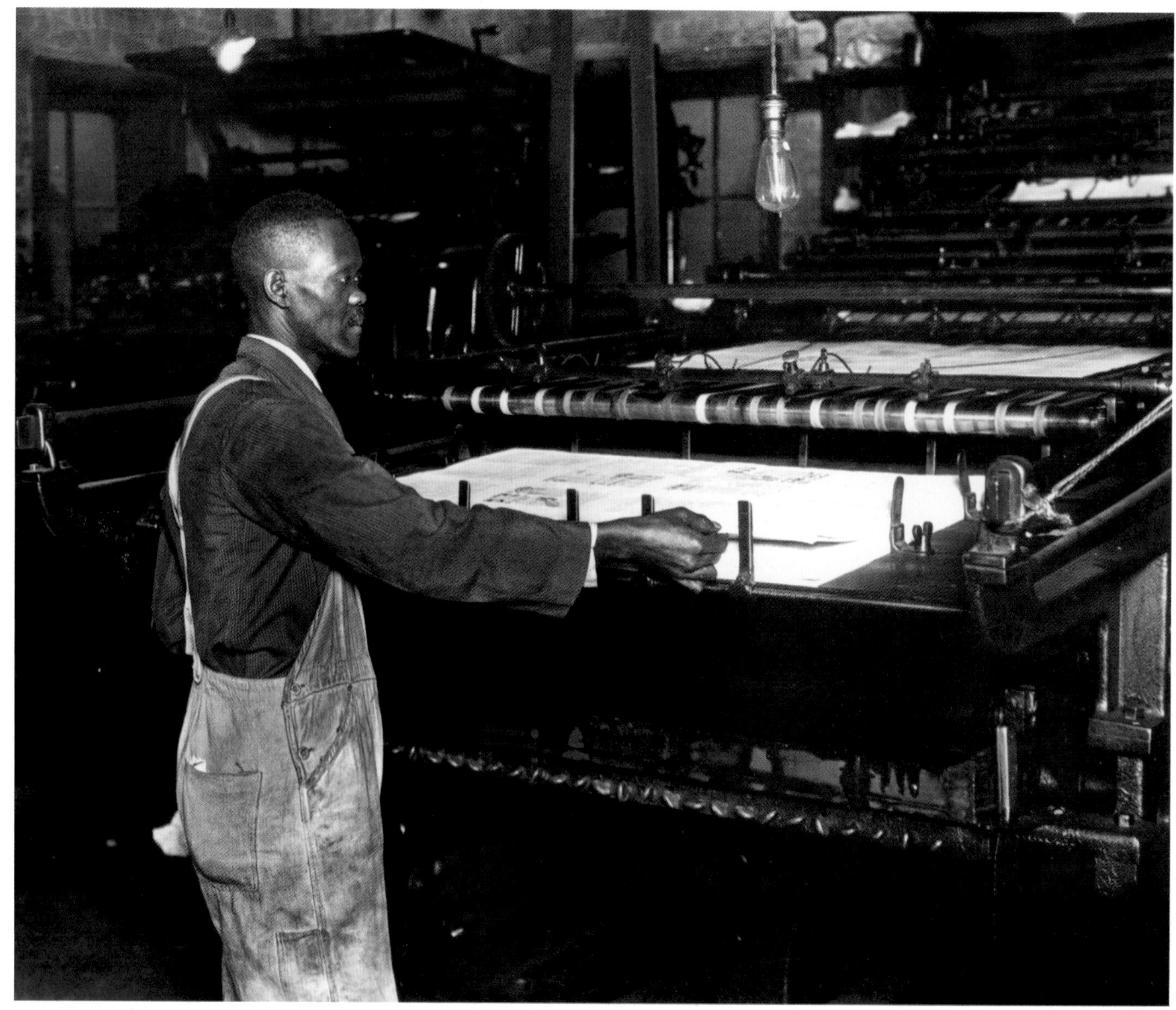

Into industry
Beginning in the 1920s, African American men and women moved increasingly into industrial jobs. A pressman adjusts pages in the printing press at a southern publishing house (above). Young women rolling tobacco leaves at a cigar factory (right).

Five

Renaissance and Depression 1920–1935

A scholarly book, documenting the history and culture of blacks in Africa and America, by the originator of *Negro History Week.*

"I am the equal of any white man. I want you to feel the same way. We have come now to the turning point of the Negro where we have changed from the old cringing weakling and transformed into full grown men demanding our portion as men."

Marcus Garvey

On March 21, 1924, Charles S. Johnson of the National Urban League hosted an elegant dinner at the Civic Club in New York. The dinner was held in honor of the publication of black writer Jessie Redmon Fauset's first novel, *There is Confusion.* But Johnson's larger purpose was to showcase black literary talent for the whites who controlled publishing, and facilitate African Americans' entry into the mainstream literary scene. Among the guests were W. E. B. Du Bois and future literary luminaries Jean Toomer, Langston Hughes, James Weldon Johnson, and Countee Cullen.

There were already indications that a new and exciting body of work would emerge from African American artists in the northern cities. Even before the turn of the century, the work of songwriter Bob Cole and composer J. Rosamond Johnson, the poetry of Paul Laurence Dunbar, the essays of Anna Julia Cooper and W. E. B Du Bois, and the fiction of Pauline Hopkins and Charles W. Chesnutt had achieved broad recognition. By the end of World War I, the fiction of James Weldon Johnson and the poetry of Claude McKay had begun to set a new tone by describing the reality of black life in America and articulating a new struggle for racial identity.

Then in the early 1920s, the black art scene was set to explode. McKay's volume of poetry, *Harlem Shadows* (1922), became one of the first works by a black writer to be published by a mainstream, national publisher. *Cane*

Previous page
A high-class lunchroom in Harlem, 1930.

(1923), by Jean Toomer, was a bold, experimental novel that combined poetry and prose to document the black experience in the rural South and the urban North. Jessie Fauset's novel, the inspiration for Charles Johnson's strategic dinner party, was an unusual depiction of black middle-class life—from a woman's perspective.

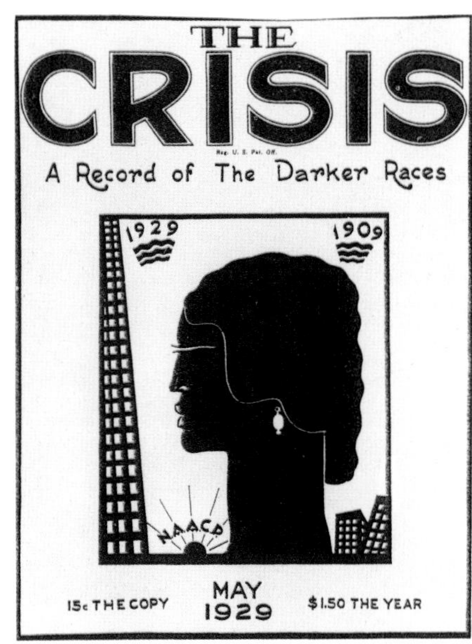

This magazine, under the editorship of W. E. B. Du Bois and produced by the NAACP, was an influential intellectual and artistic journal.

Johnson's dinner, held at a critical time, was a smashing success. Black philosopher and literary scholar Alain Leroy Locke was invited to edit an issue of *Survey Graphics*, a magazine of social analysis and criticism, and in March of 1925, the special Harlem issue hit newsstands with a blistering set of essays and poems directed at defining a unique black aesthetic and new, radical political viewpoint. Later that year, Locke expanded the issue into a book, *The New Negro*, that crystallized the artistic and intellectual movement already underway in Harlem. Locke's book and the idea of the New Negro became a milestone of American cultural history.

Charles Johnson's dinner party paid long-term dividends: In the ten years after the Civic Club gathering, some sixteen black writers published more than fifty volumes of poetry and fiction. The Harlem (or Negro) Renaissance represented a tremendous flowering of African American art—painting, music, and, particularly, literature. The artists of the renaissance were not held together by any orthodoxy of style, but united by a commitment to lend voice and value to the full range of African American experience. Langston Hughes sang the blues on the page; Claude McKay turned the sonnet to matters of justice and righteousness; Zora Neale Hurston revealed the poetry in black vernacular speech. Augusta Savage enshrined black figures in sculpture, while Aaron Douglas's paintings combined African motifs and contemporary subjects. As an intellectual as well as artistic movement, the "New Negroes" stressed the importance of recovering black history and restoring black pride.

Innovation also flourished in music. Bessie Smith and Ma Rainey sang the blues and became among the leading recording artists of the time. Jelly Roll Morton and Louis Armstrong married the blues of the rural South to the overheated pace of the city, and transformed jazz. Duke Ellington held court for an extended stay at the Cotton Club, brewing a revolution in jazz and orchestral music.

In-house magazines of the Urban League (*Opportunity*) and the NAACP (*The Crisis*) employed renaissance writers on their editorial staffs, published poetry and short stories by black writers, encouraged new work through

The 1930s writer and photographer Carl Van Vechten, who specialized in portraits of leading artistic and literary figures—African Americans in particular—and was a great patron of the Harlem Renaissance.

regular literary prizes, and broadened the black audience for literature. But the work of the Harlem Renaissance appealed to a broad spectrum of New Yorkers. The novel *Nigger Heaven* (1926), by white novelist Carl Van Vechten, helped to draw sophisticated whites to Harlem nightclubs and literary salons. Du Bois and others were critical of Van Vechten and of black novels such as Claude McKay's best-selling *Home to Harlem* (1928) for submitting to the "prurient demand[s]" of white readers and publishers for portrayals of black "licentiousness." But there was a strong and consistent insistence on the part of black writers of the right to express themselves free of constraints or expectations of either blacks or whites. This sentiment was best captured in Langston Hughes's 1926 essay *The Negro Artist and the Racial Mountain.*

The New Negro idea embraced not only the arts, but politics. The accomodationist stance of Booker T. Washington, who died in 1915, was eclipsed by the more radical ideas of the NAACP and nationalist leader Marcus Garvey's United Negro Improvement Association. Though they were bitterly divided, both organizations struck a militant tone in support of racial justice. Under the leadership of James Weldon Johnson, who was also a renaissance poet, lyricist, and novelist, the NAACP adopted the practice of hanging a banner outside the window of its Manhattan office whenever an African American was lynched. In August of 1920, Marcus Garvey presided over an unprecedented gathering of 25,000 at Madison Square Garden, in what he called the International Convention of the Negro Peoples of the World.

The New Negro philosophy of black self-determination and the relative prosperity of the years between the wars helped to create numerous black-owned businesses, from local stores and barbershops to banks and insurance companies. Many black businesses built to serve black consumers were able to thrive in an era of segregation. Madame C. J. Walker, born to Louisiana sharecroppers, built a hair-care products and cosmetics company into a thriving business, and in the process became the first self-made woman millionaire in America. Madame Walker and her daughter A'lelia Walker were, in turn, key patrons of Harlem Renaissance artists.

An NAACP flyer urging support for the Dyer Anti-Lynching Bill, 1922–23.

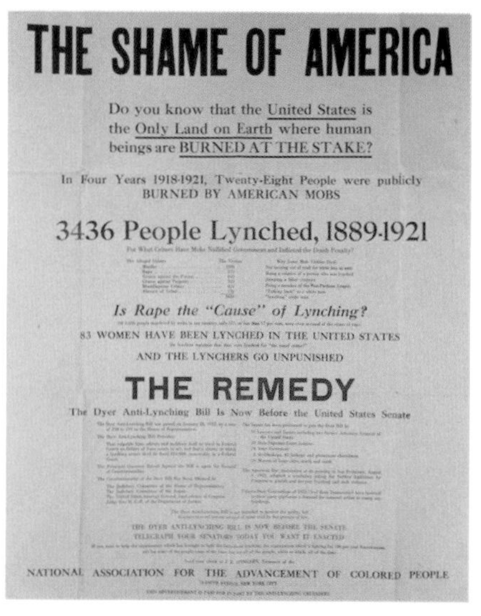

As artists and audiences came under increasing economic pressures in the Great Depression, the Harlem Renaissance declined. By the mid-1930s, black organizations had shifted their attention to the dire economic and social concerns of their constituents, and many of the leading lights of the renaissance had left New York.

Then, in March 1935, a sixteen-year-old boy was caught stealing a penknife from a white-owned shop in Harlem. The police were called, a crowd gathered, the rumors flew—and Harlem exploded in the first black riot in a major city.

After a night and day of unrest, three were dead, over a hundred injured, and a million dollars in damage was done. Harlem's image as a mecca for good times in the "jazz age" of the renaissance was over.

But the renaissance years had a lasting impact on the development of African American identity, ideology, and art. As Alain Locke argued in *The New Negro:* "If in our lifetime the Negro should not be able to celebrate his full initiation into American democracy, he can at least...celebrate the attainment of a significant and satisfying new phase of group development, and with it a spiritual Coming of Age."

Al Jolson, son of a Russian Jewish synagogue cantor, who called himself "The World's Greatest Entertainer," found fame and fortune in caricatures of African Americans. In his 1925 movie, *The Jazz Singer,* Jolson sang "Mammy" and became a star.

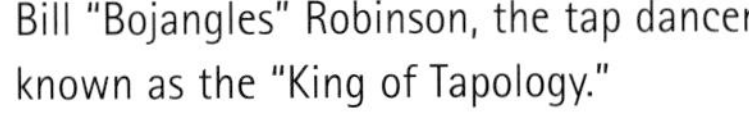

Bill "Bojangles" Robinson, the tap dancer known as the "King of Tapology."

Winners

Twelve Merit Certificate winners of the National Negro Insurance Week Contest in front of the Dunbar Mutual Insurance Society, Inc. offices in Cleveland, Ohio, c. 1930. Segregation spurred black business development: hotels, vacation resorts, transportation services, banks, and, beginning in the early twentieth century, insurance companies. Leading black companies were the North Carolina Mutual Life Insurance Company and the Atlanta Life Insurance Company, founded by barber Alonzo Herndon.

Depression years

Workers on a WPA work relief program in 1933 shift rocks as part of a landscaping project in Central Park, New York.

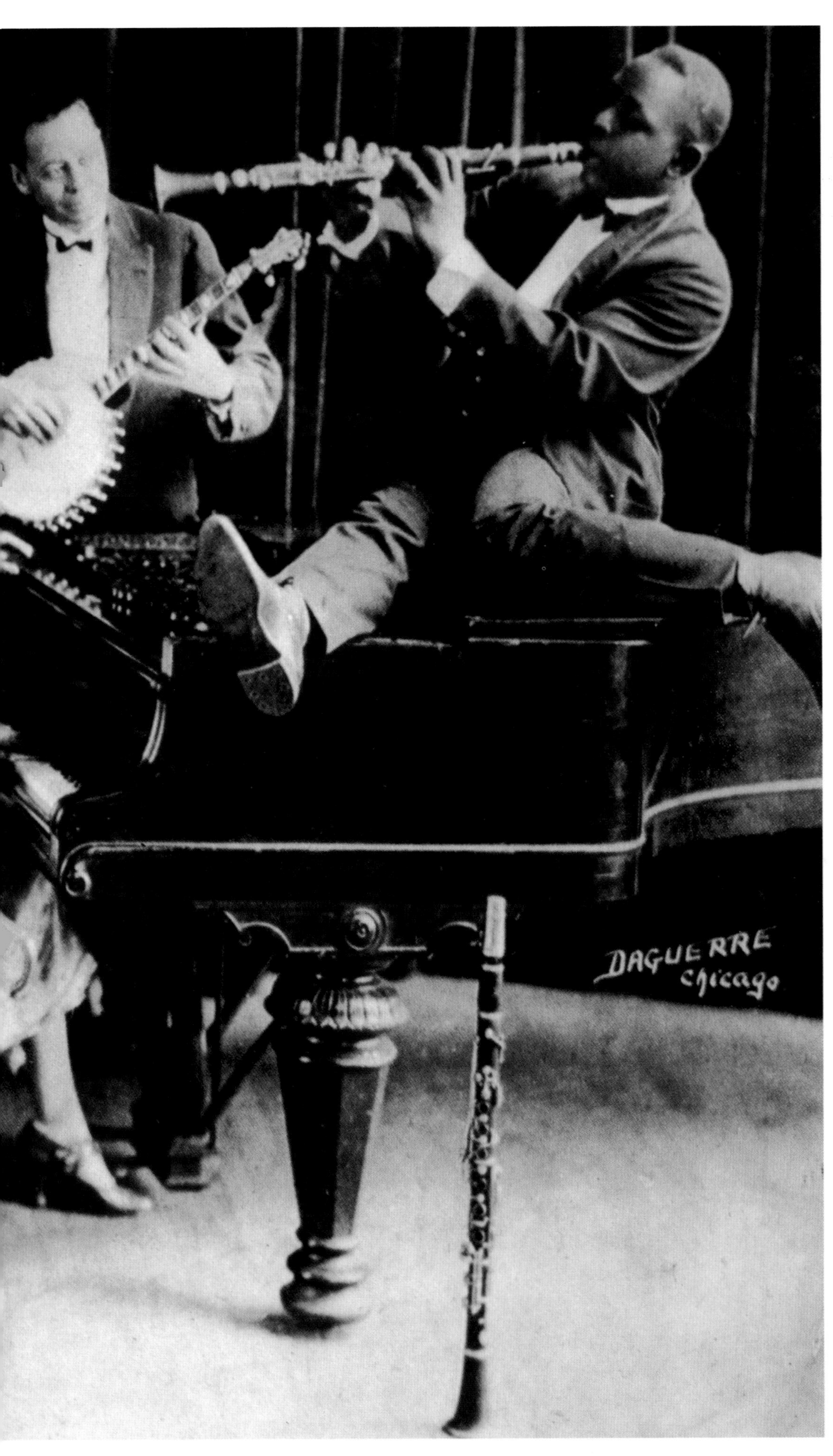

The Creole Jazz Band
This group, led by Joe "King" Oliver, was one of the most important and influential early jazz bands, here seen in Chicago in 1923, when it made a series of classic recordings. Left to right: Honore Dutrey, Baby Dodds, King Oliver (kneeling), Louis Armstrong, Lil Hardin Armstrong (his wife), Bill Johnson, and on piano, Johnny Dods. Armstrong went on to form his own group, the Hot Five, in 1925.

Jazz singers

Gertrude "Ma" Rainey (center) is regarded as one of the most influential people ever to have sung the blues. Through her wildly popular tours and over one hundred recordings, Rainey was known as the "Mother of the Blues." Here, Rainey smiles, wearing the sequined gown, headband, and ornate jewelry that were her onstage trademarks, 1923. Known as the Empress of the Blues, Bessie Smith's (left) career began when she was "discovered" by Ma Rainey. Beginning in 1923, Smith recorded with the leading jazz musicians in the country, including Louis Armstrong, James P. Johnson, and Fletcher Henderson. She was one of the most successful recording artists of her time, and her unique style continues to influence blues and jazz singers. Ivie Anderson (right) performing with Duke Ellington and his orchestra at the Palladium in London, 1933. "The Duke" is at the piano. Jazz had an established appeal in Europe well before the Second World War.

Nina Mae McKinney When she was featured in the 1929 film *Hallelujah*, directed by King Vidor and produced by MGM, Nina Mae McKinney (left) became the first black female movie star. Then, despite signing her to a five-year contract, the Hollywood studio failed to promote McKinney's career. She left the United States to tour Europe, where she became known as the "Black Garbo."

Josephine Baker, surrounded by male dancers at the Folies Bergère in Paris, 1926, at age twenty (right). She was born in St. Louis, but first came to worldwide prominence in 1925 as a singer, dancer, and cabaret performer in France. By 1927, her sleek elegance, sharp wit, and cultivated exoticism earned her more than any entertainer in Europe. She made her life in France, but remained active in the fight for African American civil rights.

COTTON CLUB
AVIS ANDREWS
ANN LEWIS
WHYTE MANIACS
The WORLD FAMOUS
COTTON CLUB
BILL ROBINSON
COTTON CLUB PARADE
DINNER $1.50
COTTON CLUB
BEAUTY SALON
DOUGHNUTS
SANDWICHES
MANICURE 35¢
PUBLIC
TAXICABS

Jam session
Jazz musicians (clockwise from top left) Artie Shapiro (bass), "Hot Lips" Page (trumpet), Coleman Hawkins (saxophone), and Joe Marsala (clarinet), at a jam session in Mamaroneck, New York, 1939. Saxophonist Willie Smith is in the background, far right.

Heart of Harlem
Harlem's Cotton Club at night, its illuminated marquee presenting Bill Robinson and Cab Calloway, New York City, c. 1932. The Cotton Club was a shimmering venue for black performers, but no African Americans could enter as customers. It is said that prominent composer W. C. Handy was once kept from crossing the threshold of the Cotton Club to hear his own music.

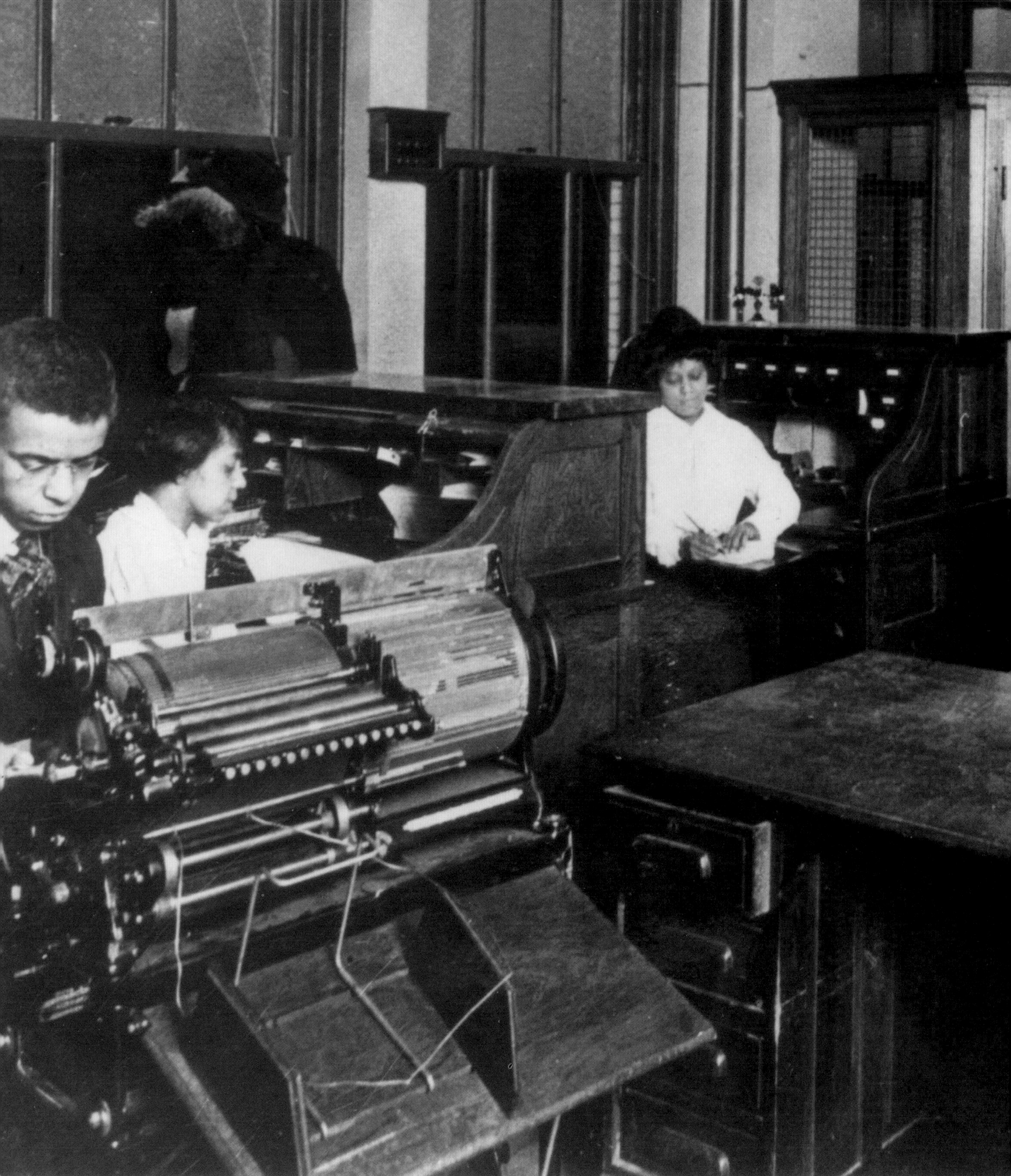

W. E. B. Du Bois (1868–1963)

Editor W. E. B. Du Bois (far right) stands in the New York headquarters of the NAACP publication *The Crisis*, his production staff hard at work at their desks, c. 1932. Du Bois, a cofounder of the NAACP, became a leading activist and writer, and one of the most influential intellectuals of the twentieth century. His increasing militance was to lead to his resignation as editor in 1934.

Lynching

A flag hanging outside the headquarters of the NAACP, c. 1938 (above). Antilynching campaigns were a primary focus of African American organizations from the 1890s through the 1940s. A crowd gathers to witness the gruesome final moments of Tom Shipp and Abe Smith in Indiana, 1930 (right). Rather than remaining shrouded in secrecy and shame, a lynching was often a public event with a festive carnival atmosphere. To white spectators, a lynching might be an evening outing fit for the whole family.

The Scottsboro Boys

In 1931, during the depths of the Depression, nine young black men, aged thirteen to twenty, were arrested and falsely accused of raping two white women on a southern railroad freight train in Alabama. The women, known prostitutes, had to be forced into saying any assault had taken place. In less than a month, eight of the defendants, who became known as the "Scottsboro Boys," were convicted and sentenced to death. Their travesty of a trial sparked popular outrage, and the support of the U.S. Communist Party in subsequent trials made the Scottsboro case into an international cause célèbre. Though all had been released by 1950, the nine defendants spent a total of more than one hundred years in prison. They eventually received an official pardon from Alabama Governor George Wallace in 1976. Only one, Clarence "Willie" Norris, was still alive. Haywood Patterson, one of the defendants, is seen in court with a lucky horseshoe (far right), and in jail on the same day (right), in April 1933, during the second trial. Three other "Boys" arrive at a Birmingham jail in 1936 (above).

Irishtown

This Brooklyn, New York, slum of pre-Civil War houses without heat, hot water, or toilets began attracting African Americans during the Depression. Many of the houses had been declared uninhabitable by the City of New York (1936).

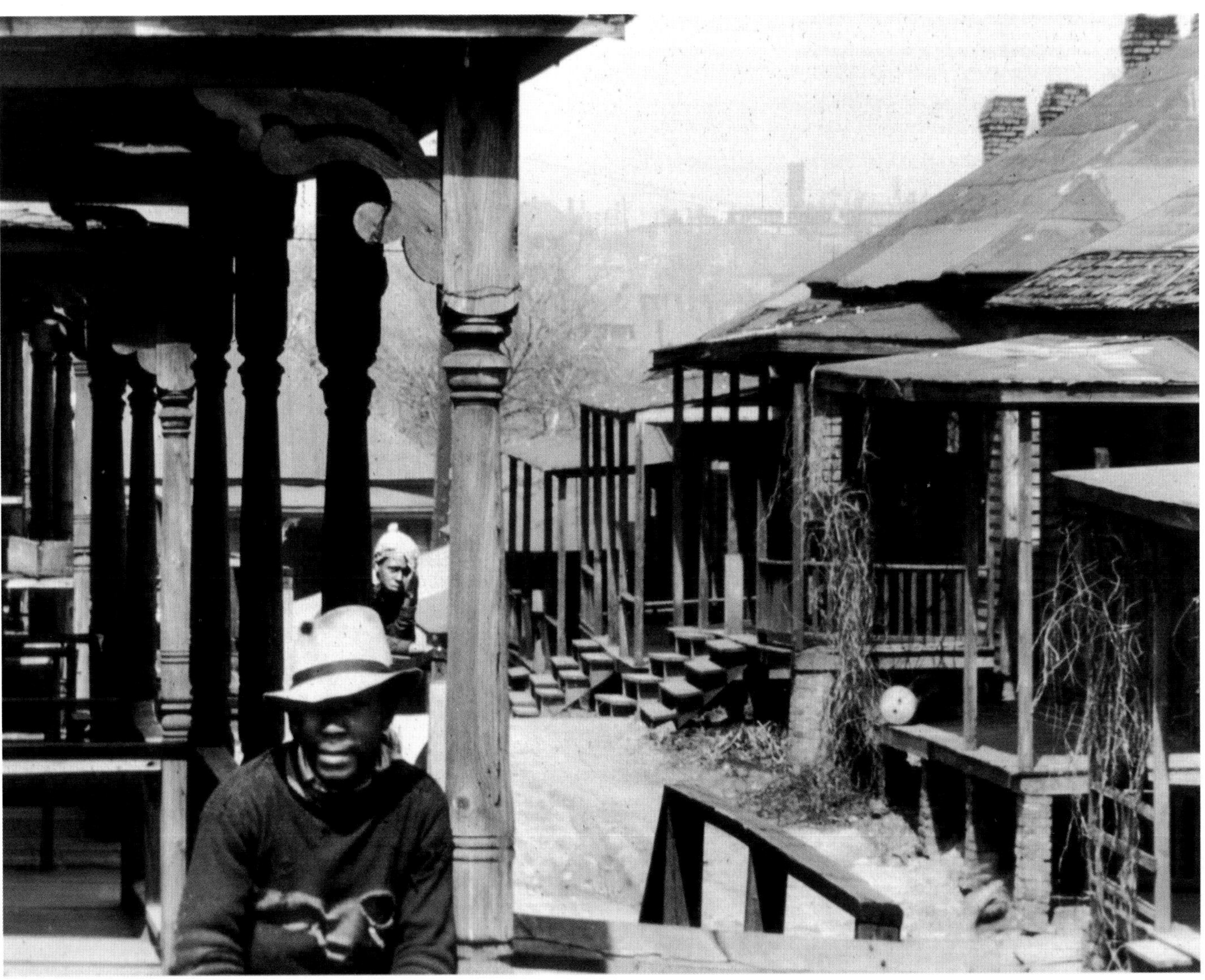

Atlanta

These houses in an African American neighborhood of the Georgia city may look more picturesque, with their timber porches, but they were probably as decrepit within as those in Irishtown (1936).

Weighing and sorting

A white planter's daughter has the privilege of checking the weight of cotton as black field hands look on, Kaufman County, Texas, 1936 (left). Jorena Pettway sorting peas inside her smokehouse in Gee's Bend, Alabama, 1939 (above). In addition to the hundreds of thousands of African Americans who fled the South in the 1910s, about another million moved north and west in the 1920s, further transforming the racial landscape of the United States. The migration was slowed by the Great Depression, but by 1940, almost a quarter of African Americans lived outside the South; even more had left rural areas for southern cities. Still, some black workers remained employed in the declining number of agricultural jobs in the South.

CBS
CBS

Bechet and Johnson

Clarinetist Sidney Bechet performing with trumpeter Bunk Johnson in Boston, 1945. Bechet was as much a master of his instrument as Louis Armstrong, but never achieved the same acclaim because in part he was no vocalist. However, when he took it up in the 1920s, Bechet was responsible for the saxophone being taken seriously for the first time. He had a shipboard romance with Josephine Baker when they were on their way to Europe in 1925. After the Second World War he lived in France permanently.

Fats Waller

Fats Waller's (left) sophisticated, witty songs and his brilliant piano playing remain firm favorites today, even though he died in 1943. It is hard to imagine "Honeysuckle Rose" or "Ain't Misbehavin' " ever being forgotten.

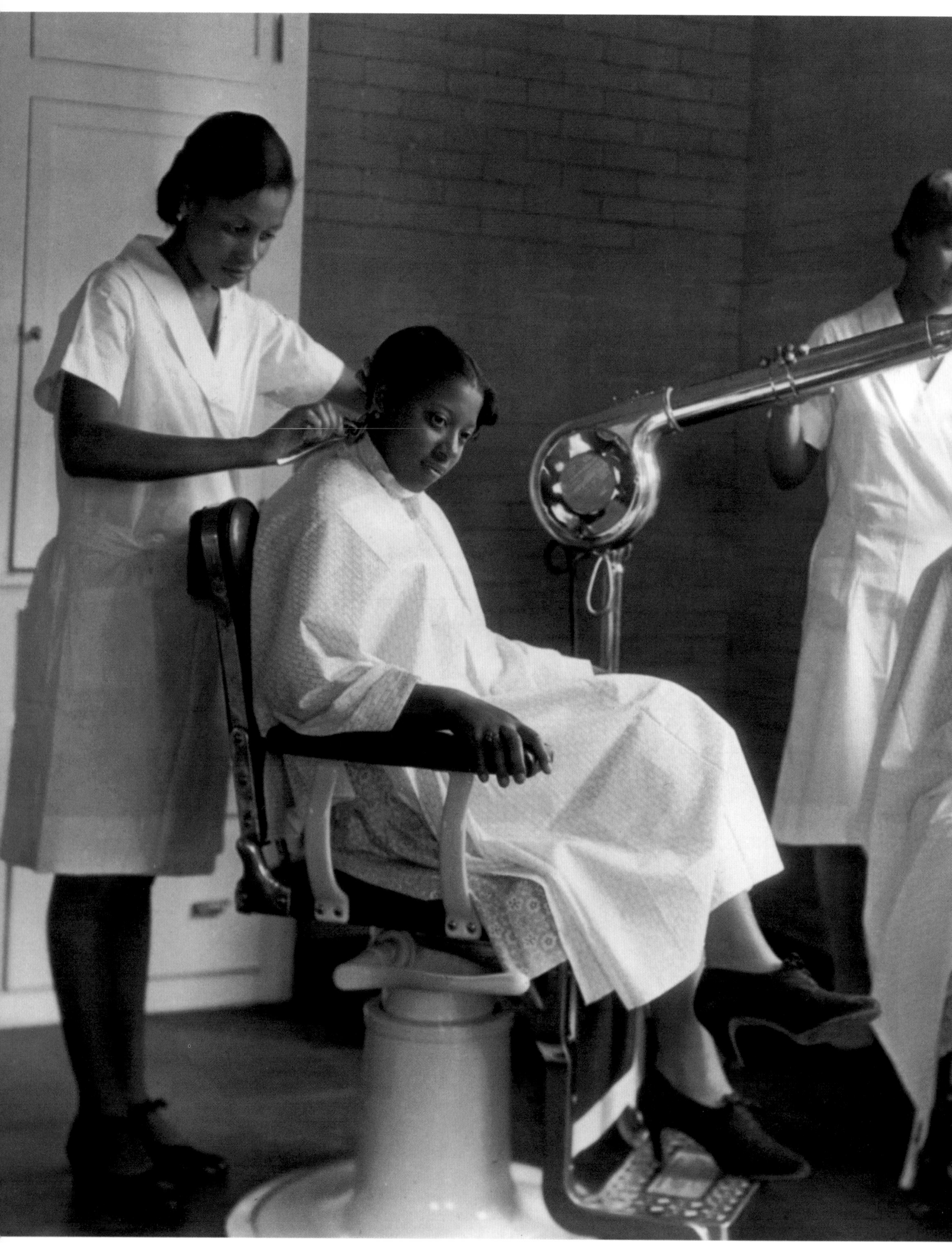

Pride in appearance
Students practice styles on one another's hair at the Bordentown School for Colored Youth, a boarding school founded by an AME minister in New Jersey, c. 1935 (left). Looking good in Kansas City, Missouri, c. 1930 (above). The most successful black entrepreneurs during the early twentieth century were Anthony Overton, Annie Minerva Turnbo-Malone, and Madame C. J. Walker. All manufactured black hair care products and cosmetics; all had sales in the millions of dollars.

Black business

Economic cooperation and the expansion of Jim Crow laws spurred the development of black-owned businesses. Between 1888 and 1934, 134 black banks were founded, including the first headed by an American woman, the St. Luke Penny Savings Bank in Richmond, Virginia. (Left) A soda fountain in a Harlem bar, c. 1935. (Above) Customers wait in line at the black-owned Dunbar National Bank in Harlem, 1933.

Harlem Renaissance I
Poet Langston Hughes, in the middle row, third from the right, sailing to Europe with the American Negro Film Group in 1932 (above). Richard Wright (left), author of *Native Son*, 1940, fell out with Zora Neale Hurston over her refusal to portray blacks as victims. Countee Cullen, using European verse forms, was the most popular black poet, until eclipsed after his death by Langston Hughes, who employed black vernacular English and rhythms (far left).

Harlem Renaissance II
Zora Neale Hurston researched black folklore before publishing *Their Eyes Were Watching God* (1938), now considered the first black feminist novel (above). James Weldon Johnson, poet novelist and editor, led the NAACP from 1920 to 1930 (right).

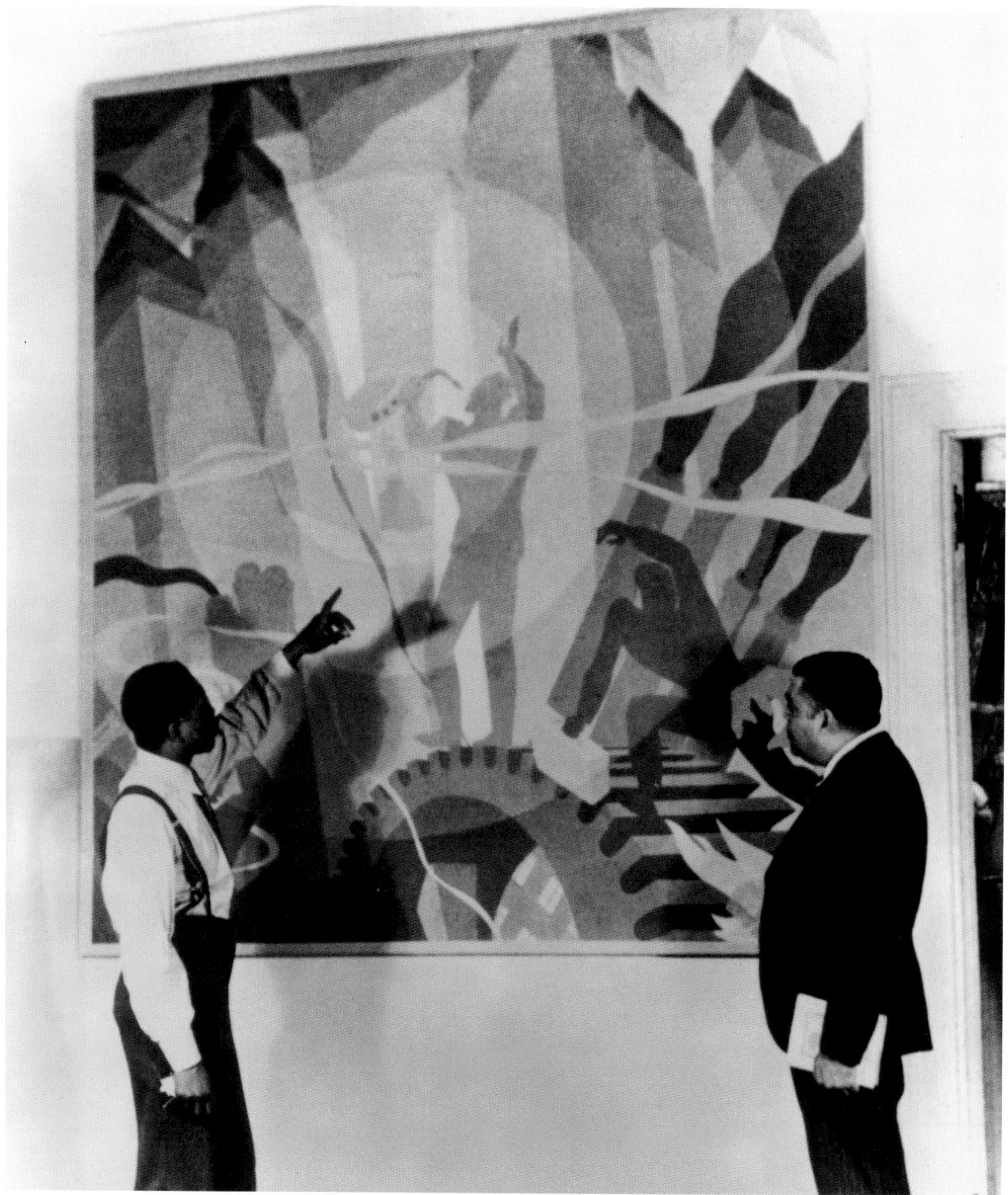

Artists

Artist Aaron Douglas and Afro-Puerto Rican book collector and curator Arthur A. Schomburg discuss Douglas's mural *Aspects of Negro Life: Song of the Towers,* 1934 (above). Douglas pioneered the incorporation of African motifs in modern painting; Schomburg established the premier collection of black books, manuscripts, and artifacts in the United States. The Florida-born Augusta Savage (right) is best remembered as a portrait sculptor of prominent black leaders, including W. E. B. Du Bois, Marcus Garvey, Frederick Douglass, and James Weldon Johnson. But Savage was also an influential teacher and mentor, leading several Harlem-based arts centers. Among her students was the prominent artist Jacob Lawrence.

PLEDGED TO
DRIVE SAFELY
19 FLORIDA 40
10-7126

Six

To the War and Beyond 1935–1950

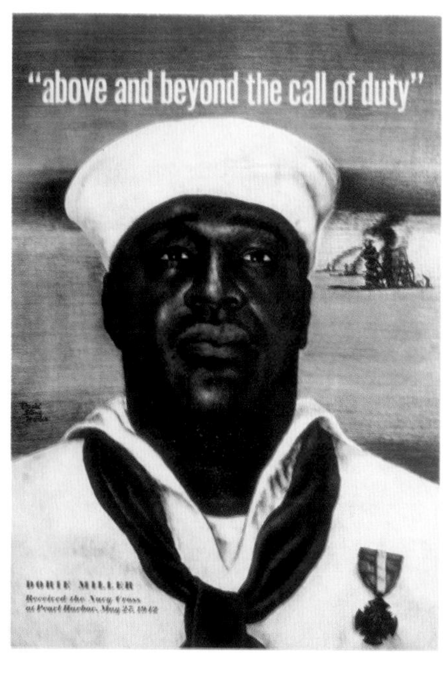

"above and beyond the call of duty"
DORIE MILLER

Naval Mess Attendant 3rd Class Doris "Dorie" Miller, wearing a Navy Cross. Miller was a crew member of the battleship USS *West Virginia*, sunk when the Japanese attacked Pearl Harbor in December 1941. He rescued wounded men and shot down four enemy aircraft, but like other African Americans, he never rose from the lower ranks.

The stock market crash of October 1929 marked the beginning of hardship for millions of Americans, and of misery for many African Americans, who were the first to feel the pain. In the cities, they quickly lost jobs after the crash; in the South, which was in a depression even before 1929, black agricultural workers were driven to the edge of starvation. By 1932, unemployment among African Americans was a staggering fifty percent. In New York, Chicago, Philadelphia, and Detroit, nearly one in every three black families had to rely on some form of public relief; in Atlanta, sixty-five percent; in Norfolk, Virginia, an amazing eighty percent. Social life declined and civic organizations stagnated.

Those African Americans who managed to keep an economic foothold came under pressure to relinquish their jobs to whites, and were subject to increased intimidation. The Ku Klux Klan enjoyed a resurgence. Lynchings of African Americans rose from seven in 1929, to twenty in 1930, and to twenty-four in 1933, the nastiest year of the Depression. In the words of contemporary journalist Hilton Butler: "Dust had been blown from the shotgun, the whip, and the noose, and Ku Klux Klan practices were being resumed in the certainty that dead men not only tell no tales but create vacancies."

Discrimination in employment was consistent with the racial segregation that divided nearly every aspect of American life. Segregation carried the full sanction of American law. The Supreme Court had ruled as far back as 1896, in *Plessy v. Ferguson,* that discrimination on the basis of race, by public or private organizations or individuals, did not violate the Constitution. Laws had subsequently been enacted in the southern states to ensure that in

Previous page
A family leaving Florida in 1940. Even at this late date, the Great Depression was having an effect.

transportation, education, public restaurants, hotels, and other accommodations, a clear and constant racial dividing line was drawn. While discrimination in the North was more often *de facto* than *de jure,* Jim Crow's reach extended to all aspects of social life in the South. Black adults were expected to show deference to whites in even the most insignificant social interactions, or face potentially violent consequences.

The New Deal, President Franklin Roosevelt's plan to lift the nation out of the economic doldrums of the Depression after his election in 1932, instituted housing, employment, agriculture, and social service programs that were unprecedented in scope. New Deal programs allowed African American farmers to purchase land, permitted some black families to purchase homes for the first time, and supported the education and training of young African Americans in a range of trades. Black writers were among those who participated in the New Deal's writing projects, and an important project to collect the narrative life histories of former slaves was begun under the Works Project Administration (WPA). But New Deal programs, as a whole, did not upset the preexisting racial hierarchy in American workplaces, organizations, and public institutions. Black farmers were likely to earn less than their white counterparts from agricultural initiatives. The National Recovery Administration permitted lower wages for African Americans than for whites doing the same work. And black families often received less than their fair share of material relief.

Ella Patterson, at 102 years old the oldest resident at the Ida B. Wells Housing Project in Chicago, Illinois, 1942 (photo: Jack Delano).

Roosevelt tolerated the perpetuation of discrimination, particularly in the early days of the New Deal, but he did expand the number of black federal appointees to unprecedented levels. The forty-five African Americans in various New Deal agencies and advisory positions by the mid-1930s became known collectively as the "Black Cabinet." Among others, the group included William Hastie in the Department of Defense, Robert C. Weaver in the Department of the Interior, *Pittsburgh Courier* publisher Robert L. Vann in the Office of the Attorney General, and Mary McLeod Bethune, founder of Bethune-Cookman College, as head of the Negro Division of the National Youth Administration.

It was not the New Deal, but the thunder of war in Europe and the U.S.'s preparations to enter World War II that began to turn the national economic tide. As the country shifted to a wartime footing, African Americans, with fresh memories of World War I, voiced increasing unwillingness to accept the segregated armed forces or discriminatory conditions that had been the norm. A group of black leaders presented President Roosevelt with a seven-

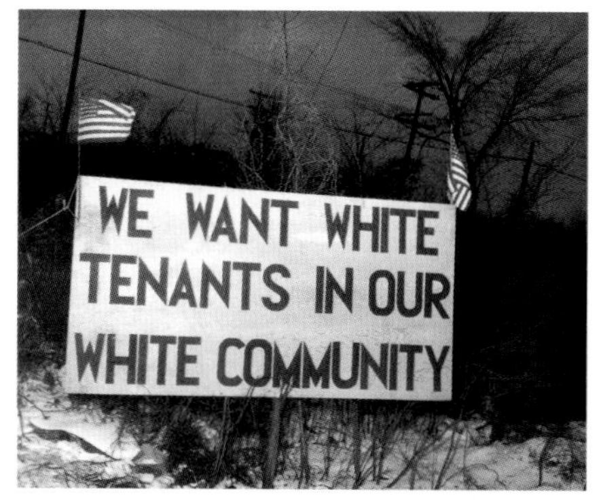

A sign placed across from the Sojourner Truth project in Detroit, Michigan in 1942 reads: "We want white tenants in our white community."

point program for equality in and integration of the armed forces. In response, Roosevelt appointed several black officials, but made no commitment to eliminating the reality of separate armies for black and white soldiers. African Americans were virtually excluded from the swelling number of jobs in the industry. Defense contractor North American Aviation, for example, announced that African Americans would be considered only for jobs "as janitors and other similar capacities.... While we are in complete sympathy with the Negro, it is against the company policy to employ them as mechanics or aircraft workers."

African Americans answered with a call for the first March on Washington. More than two decades before the better-known 1963 protest, A. Philip Randolph, President of the Brotherhood of Sleeping Car Porters, a black labor union, organized a march on the nation's capital to pressure the Roosevelt administration into ending unfair hiring practices in the expanding defense industry. The NAACP, the Urban League, and hundreds of local churches and fraternal groups joined with the Brotherhood, while Roosevelt pleaded, negotiated, and cajoled in an unsuccessful attempt to get them to call off the march. Finally, in June of 1941, Roosevelt signed Executive Order 8802, prohibiting discrimination not only in the defense industry, but throughout the federal government.

An African-American police officer in front of a "Military Police: Colored" sign, Columbus, Georgia, 1942: separate policing for a segregated army.

African Americans overwhelmingly supported the war effort. But they had first to encounter obstacles erected by their own country. Even after Roosevelt's executive order, African Americans were relegated to segregated Army units under white command, restricted to positions as messmen or laborers in the Navy, and virtually excluded from the Marine Corps and the Air Force. Northern black troops sent south for training faced violent clashes with white citizens and the hostility and condescension of white soldiers. Even the wartime blood supply was segregated.

Still, as was true in earlier military conflicts, African Americans leveraged their wartime involvement to press demands for democracy. James Thompson, a cafeteria worker from Wichita, Kansas, suggested one strategy in a letter to the *The Pittsburgh Courier*: "Should I sacrifice my life to live half American?" Thompson asked. "Will things be better for the next generation in the peace to follow? Let colored Americans adopt the 'Double V' for the double victory. The first V for victory over our enemies from without. The second V for victory over our enemies from within." The *Courier* and other African American newspapers promoted the Double-V campaign with buttons, baseball games, flag-waving ceremonies, songs—and even hairstyles.

A billboard in Dubuque, Iowa, paid for by the National Association of Manufacturers, 1940.

Despite hostility from their white counterparts, African American soldiers served in every theater of World War II. In March 1942, the U.S. Army Air Corps commissioned its first black pilots, who would be commanded by Colonel Benjamin O. Davis, Jr., and earn fame as the Tuskegee Airmen. Later that year, the Marine Corps admitted African Americans for the first time in its 144-year history, and the Army accepted the first black women into the Women Auxiliary Army Corps (WAAC). After intensive lobbying, black nurses were allowed to serve as well.

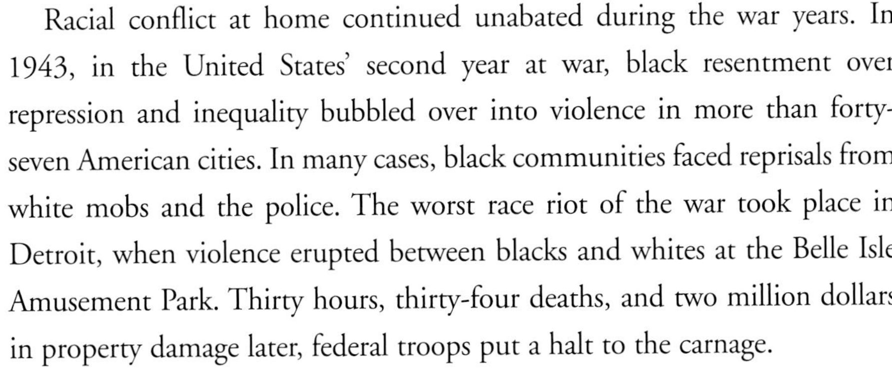

Racial conflict at home continued unabated during the war years. In 1943, in the United States' second year at war, black resentment over repression and inequality bubbled over into violence in more than forty-seven American cities. In many cases, black communities faced reprisals from white mobs and the police. The worst race riot of the war took place in Detroit, when violence erupted between blacks and whites at the Belle Isle Amusement Park. Thirty hours, thirty-four deaths, and two million dollars in property damage later, federal troops put a halt to the carnage.

"All colored cast": a 1939 film poster.

Sports became an arena for complex adjustments to American and African American identities during the war. Hitler's racist ideology had drawn the criticism of African Americans since the 1930s. Blacks took exceptional pride in the gold medals won by track star Jesse Owens and other black athletes at the 1936 Olympics, and in heavyweight boxer Joe Louis's 1938 victory over the German Max Schmeling, who was seen as a symbol of Nazism. Jackie Robinson, who was court-martialed for refusing to sit in the back of an army bus, started his career in 1945 with the Negro American Baseball League's Kansas City Monarchs. He went on to withstand the taunts of fans and the harassment of teammates to break racial barriers as a leading member of the Brooklyn Dodgers, starting in 1947.

African Americans emerged from the war years having won some significant advances, poised to push forward the ongoing struggle for equality. Membership in the NAACP surged from 50,000 in 1940 to over 400,000 six years later, with the fastest growth in the South. The Congress of Racial Equality (CORE) was founded in 1942, and staged nonviolent sit-ins in several northern cities. In many respects, the battles of the war years would pave the way for the grand upsurge in the movement for justice in the 1950s.

Waiting for work
The daily line outside the State Employment Service premises in Memphis, Tennessee, c. 1934, in the heat of the Depression. Black unemployment was twice as high as that of whites during these years.

219 203

Evicted

Sharecroppers with their families and possessions after eviction, along Highway 60 in New Madrid, Missouri, January 1939 (above and right). The Great Depression piled more hardship and misery on those already on the bottom rung of the economic ladder.

shing
SATIS
SWEET
SCOTCH
SNUFF
KOLA
Coca-Cola

Passing the time
A group out on the porch of a country store on a dirt road in Gordonton, North Carolina, July 1939. The brother of the store owner stands in the doorway of the store. One pump is for gasoline, the other for kerosene (photo: Dorothea Lange).

Work breaks

Migrant fruit pickers sit on their bunks. The grower for whom they work employs only unmarried African American men, Berrien County, Michigan, 1940 (left). A sugarcane cutter rolling a cigarette near New Iberia, Louisiana, 1938 (above).

Among the pines

Turpentine collectors in Georgia, 1937 (left), and a sawmill worker in Heard County, Georgia, 1941 (above, photos: Dorothea Lange).

Shoes

A Pullman porter contemplates the shoes arrayed outside curtained sleeping compartments, c. 1935 (left). From the time of its founding shortly after the Civil War, the Pullman Company had hired African Americans exclusively as porters and maids for its famed sleeping cars. As rail travel burgeoned in the 1920s, the company became the largest single employer of black workers. This porter was likely to be a member of the Brotherhood of Sleeping Car Porters, an all-black union founded in 1925 by A. Philip Randolph. The Brotherhood grew into a critically important and influential organization. Two young shoe-shine entrepreneurs outside the famous New York jewelry store, Tiffany & Co., c. 1940 (right).

TIFFANY & CO.
15¢

HOLY BIBLE
422
MAY'S & JOHNSO
BEAUTY SCHOO
BONAPARTE SYST
HAIR CUT 25¢
SHAVE 15¢
JONES BARBER SHOP
HAIR CUT 25¢
15¢
424
SHAVE 15¢

Harlem street scene
Businesses on the 420 block of Lenox Avenue in Harlem, New York City, 1938. The building on the left has become one of the many small black places of worship in the area.

The plantation store

Day laborers waiting to be paid and to buy supplies inside a plantation store on a Friday night, Marcella Plantation, Mississippi Delta, 1939. Black workers who remained in the South during the days of the Great Migration suffered the most devastating impact of the Depression years, when cotton prices plummeted and agricultural jobs disappeared.

Tobacco auction
A black farmer talking with the warehouse man about the price he received at auction for his tobacco, Durham, North Carolina, 1939.

Hair care

The Two Sisters beauty salon, furnished and equipped in a thoroughly up-to-date way, with the staff in uniform, c. 1940.

Barbershop
A much less sophisticated men's equivalent in Vicksburg, Mississippi, 1936, although it also served as a meeting place and unofficial social club.

Jim Crow laws

The stairs to separate seating in a Mississippi cinema (above). Another Mississippi town has a blacks-only cinema (left). In Durham, North Carolina, (top right) when using public transport there are separate waiting rooms for those who will later sit in different parts of the bus, just as a café has separate sections and doors (bottom right). Ironically, the need for separate establishments allowed some independence to black entrepreneurs, and the humiliations of public transport also spurred blacks to buy their own cars.

COLORED
WAITING ROOM
PRIVATE PROPERTY
NO PARKING
Driving through or Turning Around
BINGO
TONITE!
Good
Housekeeping
True Story
HITLER'S
LOVE LIFE
REVEALED
COACH COMPANY
45

WHITE
COLORED
FARMERS CAFE
QUICK LUNCH
HOT
WEINERS
HAMBURGERS
5¢
LUNCHES
BYRD BRO
FIELD GARDEN

Colored water
A segregated drinking fountain in Oklahoma City, 1939.

WHITE
MEN
COLORED
COLORED

Racial barriers

The partition down the middle of the cinema (above) is unusual. Normally African Americans sat upstairs. Black workers (right) leaving a shipyard in Beaumont, Texas, in 1943 have to keep to one side of the barrier, visible bottom right. Federal Government efforts to ensure nondiscrimination in war industries were to provoke riots in Beaumont that year.

Boys club boxing
Boxing and sports in general offered opportunities and the promise of glory for many young African Americans. These two young men, who may have been inspired by heavyweight champion Joe Louis, "the Brown Bomber," are watched by other black teenagers in the New Haven Boys Club, Connecticut, 1935.

Jesse Owens

Jesse Owens (1913–1980), on the far right, at the start of a race at the 1936 Olympic Games (left). When Adolf Hitler tried to use the 1936 Olympics in Berlin to demonstrate Aryan superiority, black track star Jesse Owens was America's rebuttal. Owens took gold medals in the 100 and 200 meter races, the long jump, and the 400 meter relay. In all but one of these events, Owens set Olympic records. He was welcomed home with much fanfare, but soon had to contend again with American racism. "After I came home," Owens would later say, "it became increasingly apparent that everyone was going to slap me on the back, want to shake my hand, or have me up to their suite. But no one was going to offer me a job." Owens is pictured just after breaking a world record while still in high school, Cleveland, Ohio, 1932 (top).

"Mammy"
Hattie McDaniel in her Academy Award–winning role as "Mammy," tightening Vivien Leigh's corset in *Gone With the Wind*. Despite her prodigious talent, McDaniel was largely limited to playing maids; her Hollywood studio contract even forbade her from losing weight. Faced with vigorous criticism from black organizations for playing parts that perpetuated racial stereotypes, McDaniel said, "I'd rather make $700 a week playing a maid than earn $7 a day being a maid."

"De Lawd"
Rex Ingrams as "De Lawd" in the 1936 film *Green Pastures*, based on a play of the same name. The play and the movie were written by white men. Though lauded for the use of African American spirituals, the film was heavily criticized for caricatured black dialect and stereotyped characterizations.

Marian Anderson
The Daughters of the American Revolution would not let the prominent contralto (right) perform in Constitution Hall in Washington in 1939. President Roosevelt's wife, Eleanor, resigned from the Daughters in protest, and the Secretary of the Interior arranged for an open-air concert on Easter Sunday at the Lincoln Memorial. It was attended by 75,000 people (above).

KKK

The fiery cross
One of the Ku Klux Klan's symbols. The Klan had been virtually refounded in 1915 and thereafter was actually strongest outside the South, especially in Indiana. It targeted Roman Catholics, Jews, and ne'er-do-wells, as well as African Americans.

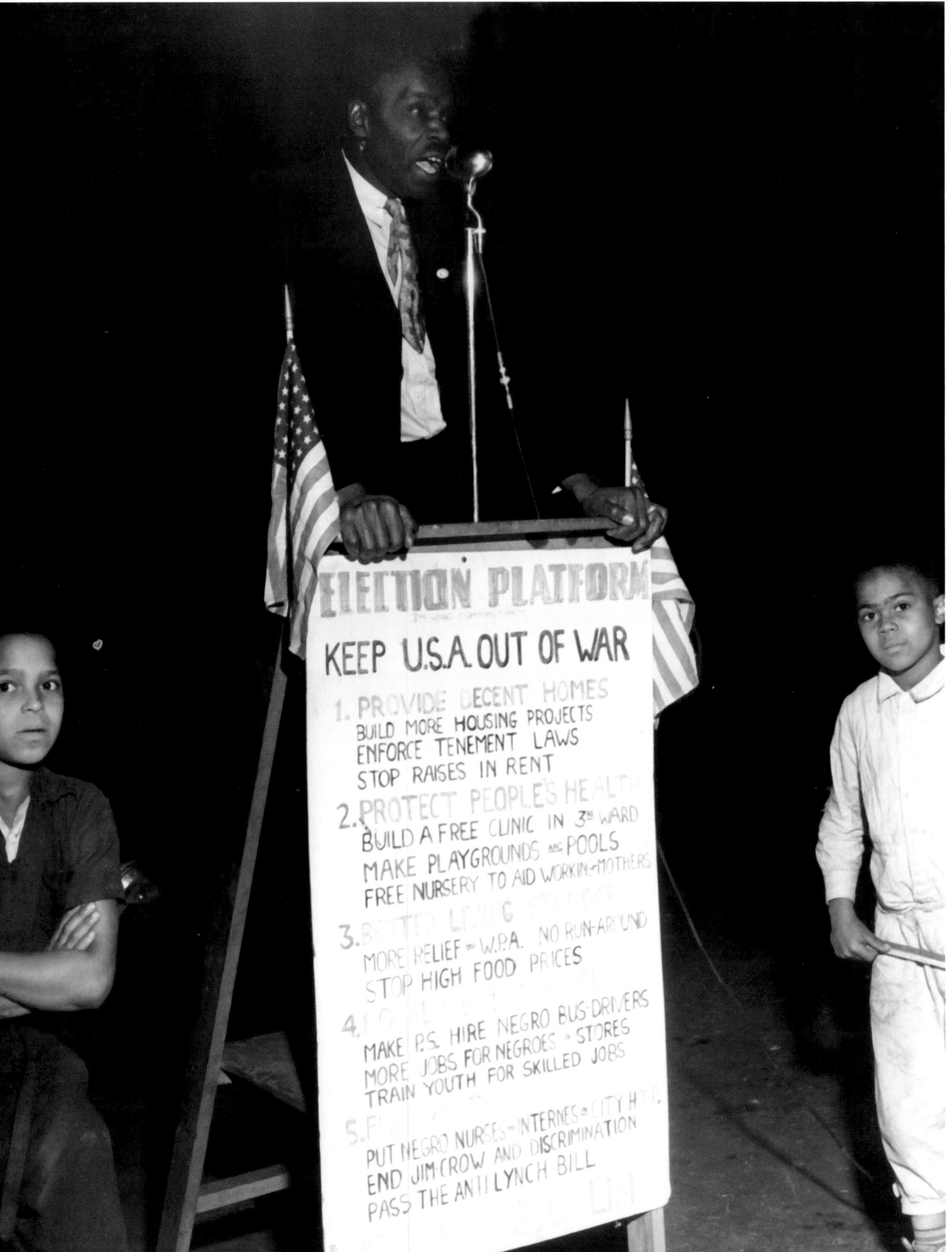
ELECTION PLATFORM
KEEP U.S.A. OUT OF WAR
1. PROVIDE DECENT HOMES
BUILD MORE HOUSING PROJECTS
ENFORCE TENEMENT LAWS
STOP RAISES IN RENT
2. PROTECT PEOPLE'S HEALTH
BUILD A FREE CLINIC IN 3RD WARD
MAKE PLAYGROUNDS AND POOLS
FREE NURSERY TO AID WORKING MOTHERS
3.
MORE RELIEF & W.P.A. NO RUN-AROUND
STOP HIGH FOOD PRICES
4.
MAKE P.S. HIRE NEGRO BUS-DRIVERS
MORE JOBS FOR NEGROES IN STORES
TRAIN YOUTH FOR SKILLED JOBS
5.
PUT NEGRO NURSES & INTERNES IN CITY
END JIM-CROW AND DISCRIMINATION
PASS THE ANTI LYNCH BILL

Platform

Demands for African Americans to join the war effort provoked debate among blacks about their place in U.S. society, and provided an opening for blacks to press their own demands. (Left) a speaker supporting the Communist party's platform opposing U.S. entry into the war. (Right) black military service, as suggested in this placard, was a powerful argument against segregation.

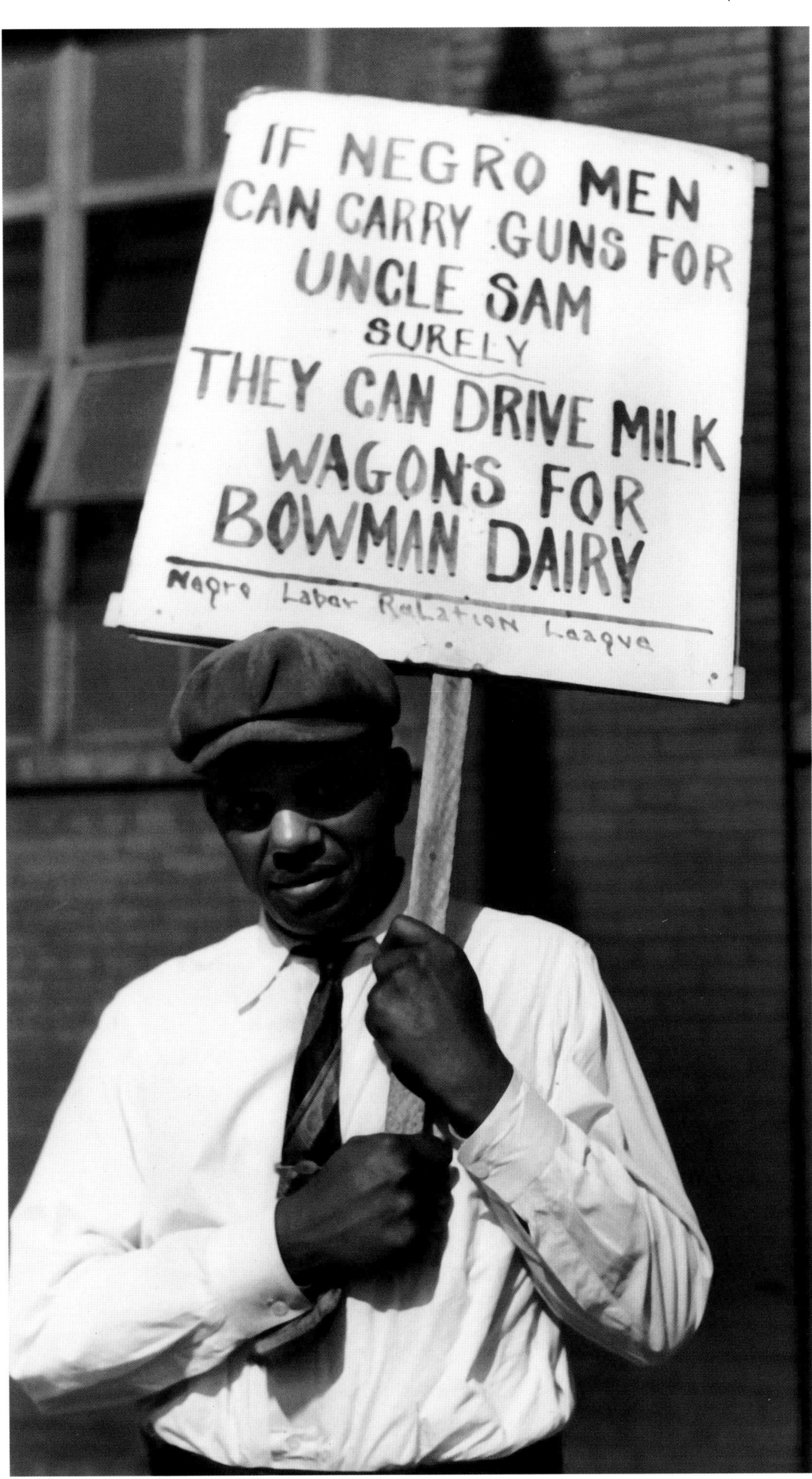

Burmese mud

A convoy of jeeps and trailers, manned by African American troops, has gotten itself firmly bogged down somewhere in the Burma jungle in 1944. The chains attached to the wheels have obviously had little effect.

Paratroopers
A white instructor checks a parachute and harness before these black recruits make a training jump, Fort Benning, Georgia, 1944.

Army, Navy
Naval recruits at Manhattan Beach Training Station, Brooklyn, New York, 1943 (right). Soldiers of the 41st Corps of Engineers, an African American unit, parade at Fort Bragg, North Carolina, 1942.

NAB POLICE SLAYER MISSING 6 MONTHS
Chicago Defender
CITY EDITION
CITES SAILOR FOR HEROISM
CHICAGOANS FIGHT WITH
IN AUSTRALIA
CABLE KIN OF SAFE ARRIVAL AT WAR SCENE
LIB

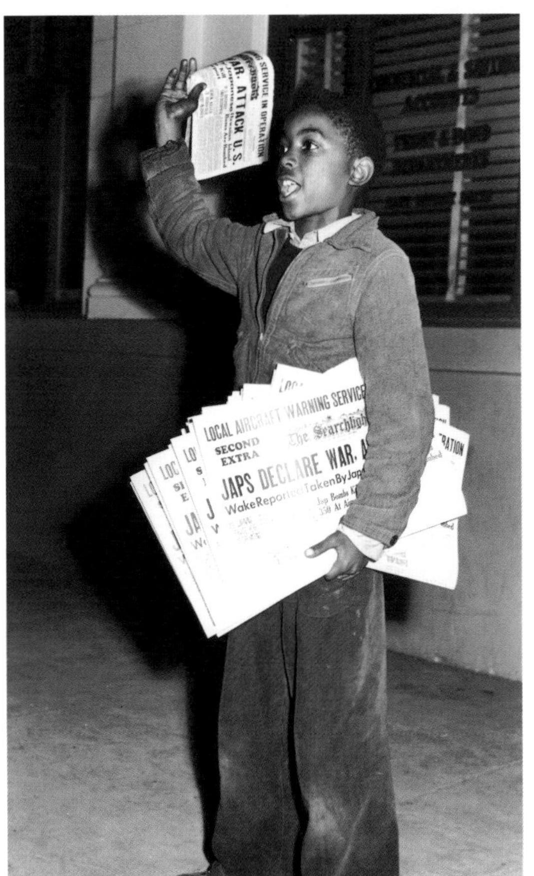

Headlines

A man is reading the papers on his bed in Memphis, Tennessee, in November 1941—one has a headline about fighting a Jim Crow law (above). Soon the headlines will change dramatically. A news vendor (left) sells papers in Redding, California, announcing the Japanese attack on Pearl Harbor, 1941. Another newsboy (far left) is selling the *Chicago Defender* in April 1942. The headline tells us that General MacArthur has been forced out of the Philippines by the Japanese and is regrouping in Australia.

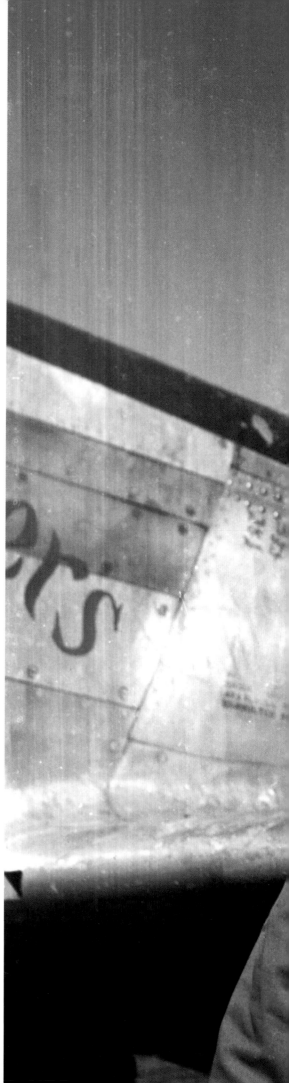

Father and son
General Benjamin O. Davis, Sr. (above), with members of an Engineer firefighting service at their base in France, 1944. In 1940, Davis became the first African American general officer in the history of the U.S. Armed Forces. His son, Benjamin O. Davis, Jr. (right), who died on the Fourth of July, 2002, was the first African American of the century to graduate from West Point U.S. Military Academy and the first commander of the famed Tuskegee Airmen, an all-black corps of fighter pilots. Under Davis's command, the airmen didn't lose a single bomber escorted to enemy fire during 200 World War II missions.

Captain
Hugh Mulzac, an immigrant from the West Indies, had earned his captain's rating in the merchant marine and had worked as a ship's captain for Marcus Garvey's Black Star Line. In 1942, Captain Mulzac became the first black officer to command an integrated crew.

INSP-10-6-
B.O. DAV

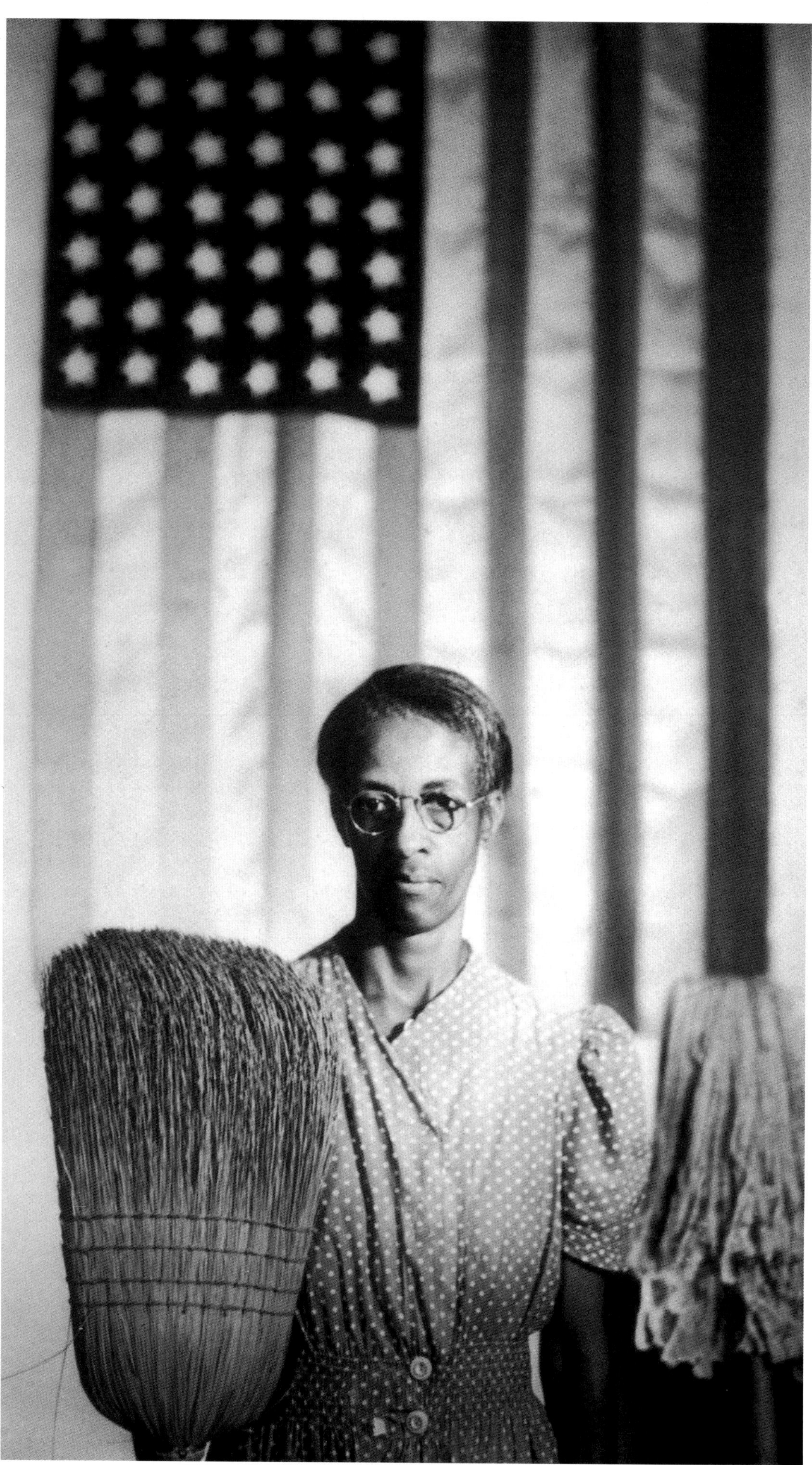

Servants of government
Ella Watson (left), a charwoman working in government offices in Washington, D.C., in 1942 is seen posing in a bit of wartime propaganda doing her duty for her country with mop and broom. Less ironically, Mary McLeod Bethune was photographed in her office in 1943. Bethune, founder of the National Council of Negro Women and of Bethune-Cookman College, was organizer of Roosevelt's Federal Council on Negro Affairs, informally known as the "Black Cabinet." After the war, Bethune, with W. E. B. Du Bois and Walter White, was a delegate to the organizing meeting of the United Nations. In 1974, she became the first woman and first African American to be honored with a public statue in Washington, D.C.

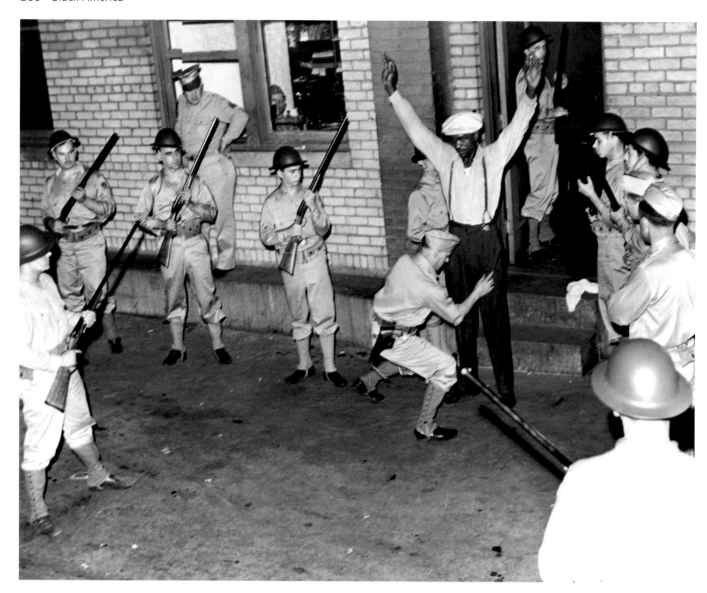

Detroit riots, 1943

Racial tension flared up as blacks and whites vied for housing and jobs. A mother (far right) tries to prevent the arrest of her fourteen-year-old son in June outside the Sojourner Truth Homes, built by the federal government for blacks but later turned over to whites. Cars burn in the street (right). Order was restored after thirty hours when military police were sent in (above). There had been reluctance to interfere by the federal government in case this was seen as a sign of weakness by Japan and Germany.

War effort

An African American war worker in a munitions factory (above). Workers assemble parts in a bomber plane production plant (left), 1942. An African American firefighter enjoys a coffee break with his coworkers, 1945 (above right). Instructor Elmer House (right) listens to a recitation by members of his first aid class, in an air warden unit in Washington, D.C., November 1942. After one year of war, U.S. arms production equaled the total of Germany, Italy, and Japan combined.

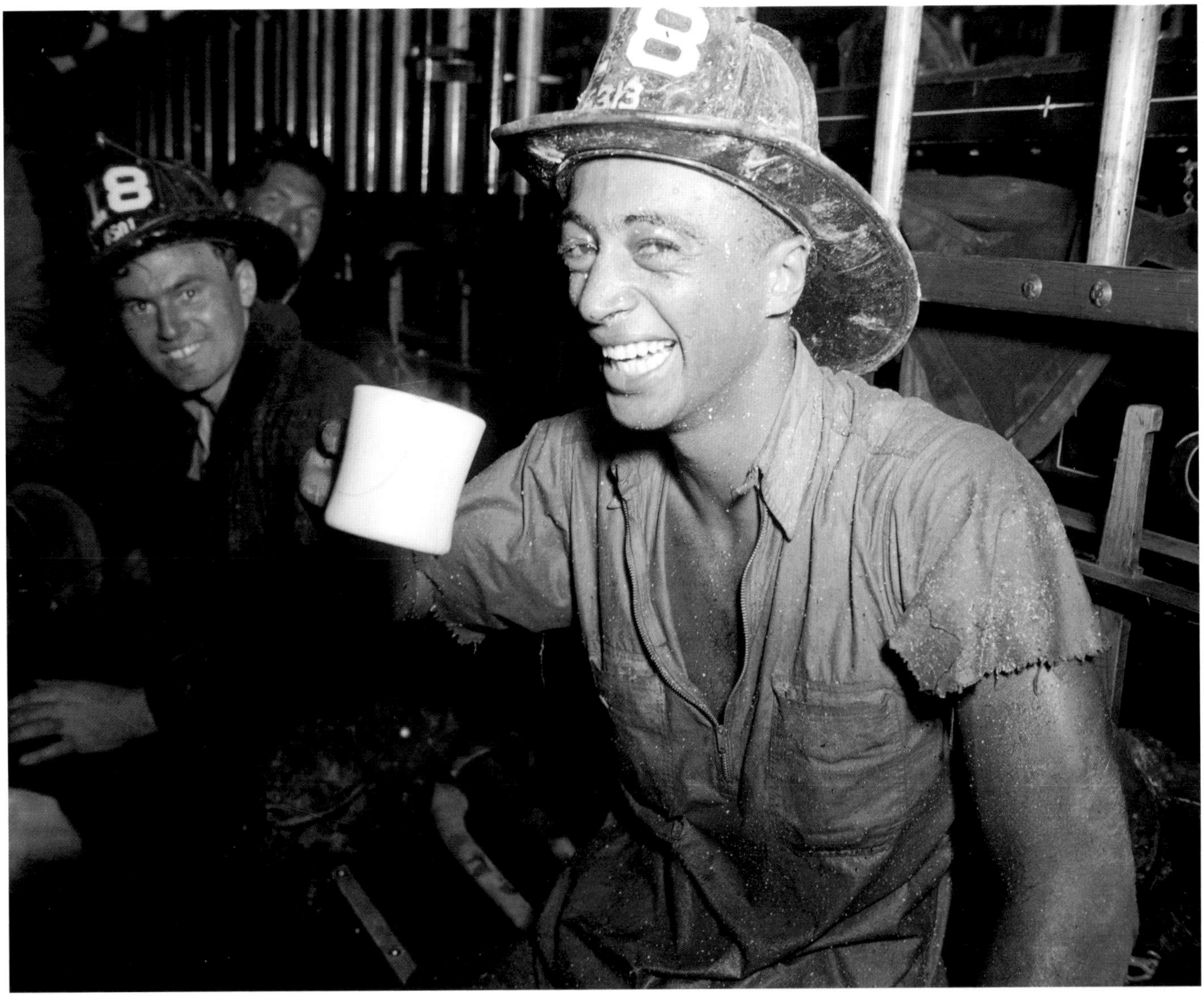

Take your place in
CIVILIAN DEFENSE

Doing their bit

The college-educated baseball player and outstanding all-around athlete Jackie Robinso doing his basic training for th army (left). Joe Louis, heavyweight boxing champion the world 1937 to 1949, does battle training (below). Only a Louis intervened was Jackie Robinson made an officer. The singer, actor, and activist Paul Robeson sings the "Star Spang Banner" with shipyard workers Oakland, California, Septembe 1942 (right).

Allies again
French soldiers distribute handfuls of candy to black GIs in celebration of the closing of the Colmar Pocket Battle, February 5, 1945. The Colmar Pocket was an area into which the Germans had been hemmed, leaving them only two bridges across which to retreat over the Rhine back to Germany.

War's ending

A woman loses herself in her dancing as she celebrates in a Harlem nightclub (above). New Yorkers toss bundles of ticker tape, thrown earlier from surrounding skyscraper windows, during a victory parade in 1945.

SANDWICHES
Aloha
TROPICAL DRINKS

Middle-class aspirations

African American families pose proudly inside and outside their homes, with the trappings of material success around them. The images are intended to convey that they, too, have shared in the prosperity that came with the huge surge in manufacturing that followed the outbreak of war. Norman Rockwell's visions of decent, genial middle America, used as covers for the *Saturday Evening Post* for several decades, can encompass them, too.

Books and a beer

The March Community Bookshop in Harlem, 1940 (above), and the customers in a Chicago tavern in 1941 (right) speak clearly of the aspirations and achievements of African Americans in the big northern cities.

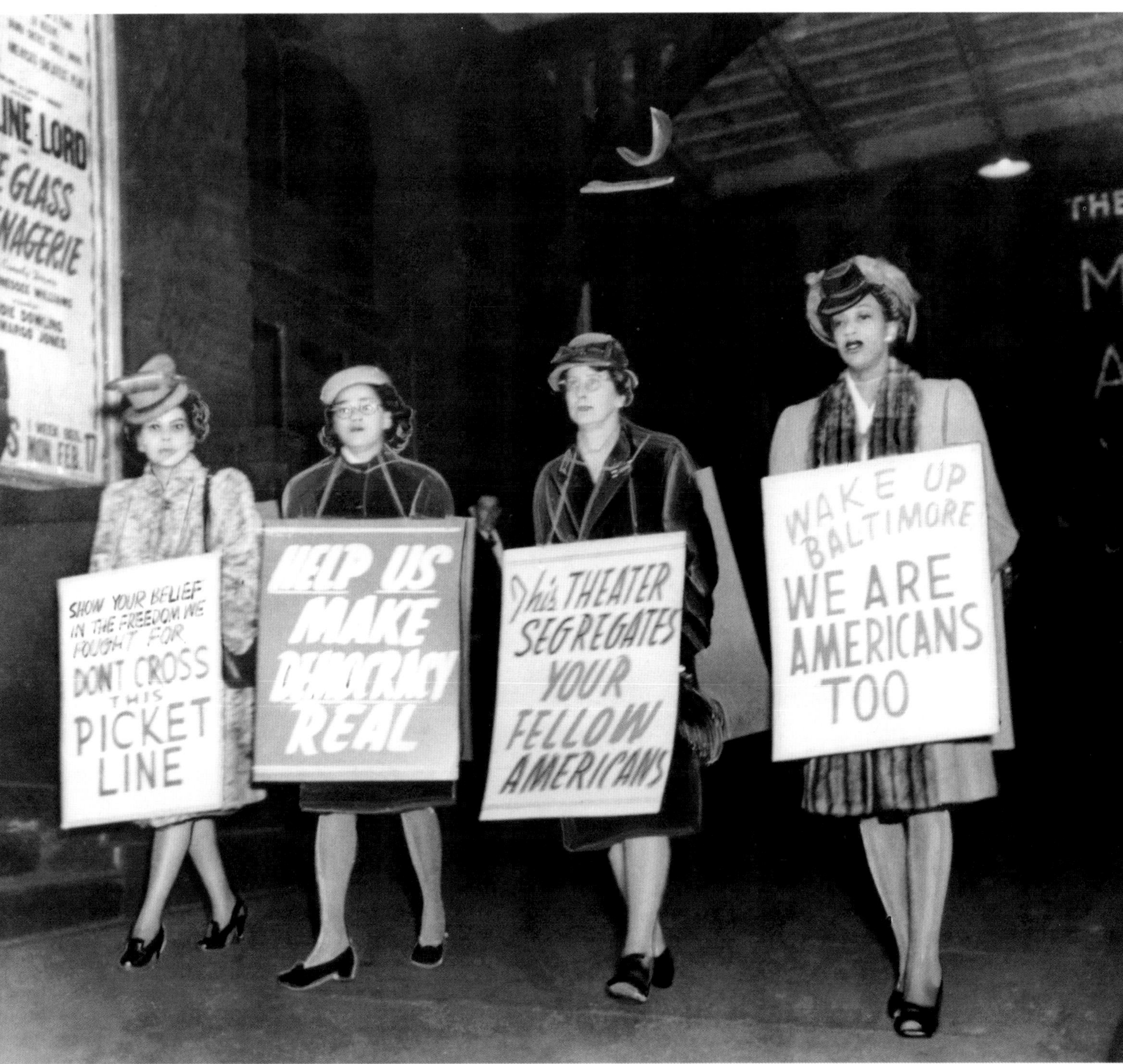

Riot or change

A victim of riots in Columbia, Tennessee, lies on the ground as police, pistols in hand, stoop over him (left), February 1946. Four members of the NAACP picket a segregated theater in Baltimore, where Tennessee Williams's play *The Glass Menagerie* is showing, c. 1946 (above).

48

Jackie Robinson
While at UCLA, he emerged as a wonderful all-around athlete, playing football, basketball, and baseball, and holding the national long jump record. He began his professional baseball career with the Kansas City Monarchs of the Negro League in 1945 (above). In 1947, he played for the Brooklyn Dodgers (left), the first African American in the major leagues since Moses Fleetwood Walker in 1883. This paved the way for blacks in all other professional team sports.

Jazz composers
Duke Ellington, pianist and bandleader, is also acknowledged as the greatest jazz composer of all time. He is seen (right) onstage in Paris in 1958. His band was a staple at Harlem's Cotton Club from 1927 to 1931, when broadcasts and recordings brought national fame. Such compositions as "Mood Indigo" and "It Don't Mean a Thing If It Ain't Got That Swing" were fruits of this period. From the early 1940s, Ellington started producing a series of ambitious large-scale works. Listening to a late-night Ellington broadcast in 1939 got Charles Mingus (left) hooked on jazz. He became a virtuoso bass player and, like Ellington, an outstanding composer, going back to the blues and reviving collective improvisation, as well as introducing a degree of dissonance, thereby anticipating the free jazz of the 1960s.

Billie Holiday
A jazz legend, whom Frank Sinatra was to call his greatest single musical influence. The ravages of her personal life combined with her huge interpretative skills to give her performances an enormous emotional charge. "Strange Fruit," an antilynching song, became her signature piece.

Carmen McRae
Much influenced by Billie Holiday, she made her first solo recordings in 1953–54. Here she is seen performing at the New York Jazz Festival in 1957. As a result of her international tours, she became especially popular in Japan.

Pearl Bailey

Singer, actress, and entertainer, on the stage, on TV, and in such films as *Carmen Jones* (1955), *That Certain Feeling* (1956) and *Porgy and Bess* (1959).

Eartha Kitt

She performs here in her "sex kitten" mode at London's Leicester Square Odeon in 1957, though she was much more associated with nightclubs and cabarets, which were better suited to her sophisticated style of singing.

Count Basie

Pianist and big-band leader, he, as much as white clarinetist Benny Goodman, was entitled to call himself "King of Swing."

Satchmo
Louis Armstrong, the consummate entertainer and world-class star, plays his audience as well as his trumpet on a British tour.

Ella and Dizzy

The saxophone lineup in Dizzy Gillespie's Big Band, c. 1945 (above). For some he was an even greater trumpeter than Louis Armstrong. He was also responsible for introducing Afro-Cuban influences to the American jazz scene and, together with Charlie Parker, developing bebop, or modern jazz. Ella Fitzgerald (left, in 1952) began as a singer in the swing era, but effortlessly moved into bebop. Once there, however, she was able to modify its angularity, making it more accessible without losing sophistication. She was the "queen of scat," singing nonsense words and sounds to mimic instruments. Her 1950s interpretations of Porter, Ellington, and Gershwin songs are some of the most successful recordings ever.

Seven

The Era of Civil Rights 1950–1972

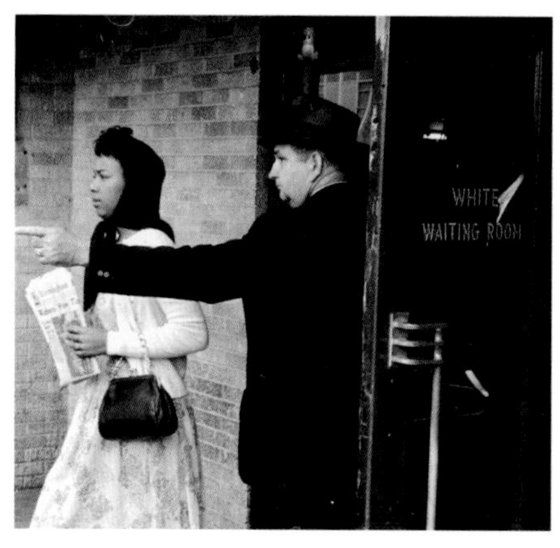

A black woman is ordered out from a whites-only waiting room in Dallas, Texas, 1961.

In the years after World War II ended, the movement for justice and equality for African Americans gained momentum. Along with other civil rights organizations, the NAACP continued to broaden its base of support as the group's legal arm, headed by Thurgood Marshall, pursued a methodical litigation strategy toward dismantling segregation. In 1954, the nascent movement won its first major victory when the U.S. Supreme Court, in a landmark decision, struck down segregation in public schools in the case *Brown v. Board of Education of Topeka, Kansas.* Events unfolded rapidly thereafter, with the movement gaining momentum and leaders accumulating experience in a span of several years.

In August of 1955, months after the *Brown* decision, fourteen-year-old Emmett Till was brutally murdered while visiting relatives in Mississippi. After his mother insisted upon an open-casket funeral, 50,000 people viewed young Emmett's battered body in Chicago; millions more were sickened by photos published in magazines and newspapers around the world. The Till murder and the subsequent acquittal of his killers by an all-white jury created an international outcry against southern injustice.

The sentiment generated by the Emmett Till murder fed the Montgomery Bus Boycott, which began only three months later. Rosa Parks, a civil rights activist, refused to relinquish her seat to a white man, as required under Alabama's segregation laws. In a yearlong protest, eventually led by Rev. Martin Luther King, Jr., African Americans faced firebombings, sniper fire, police harassment, and overwhelming white hostility. But they emerged victorious when the Supreme Court declared segregation on buses to be unconstitutional. In the wake of the boycott, ministers from Montgomery

Previous page
Martin Luther King, Jr., held in an armlock by a policeman as he is checked into jail in Montgomery, Alabama, while his wife Coretta looks on, September 1958. His "offense" was to have lingered on the steps of the courthouse. When King faced fourteen days in jail for refusing to pay a fourteen-dollar fine, the local police commissioner paid it to deny him any publicity.

and around the south founded the Southern Christian Leadership Conference (SCLC) in 1957 and elected Martin Luther King, Jr., president.

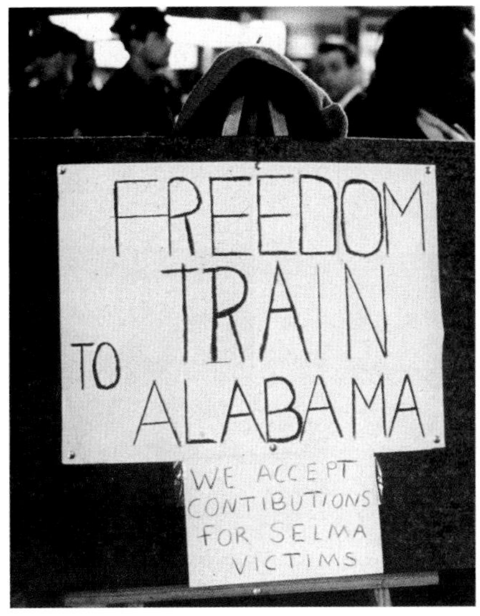

Collecting funds for the 3,000 African Americans jailed in Selma, Alabama, in 1965 for supporting a campaign for voting rights.

There were other reasons that 1957 was a milestone year. When a group of black parents in Little Rock, Arkansas, won a court order mandating the admission of black students to Central High School, Governor Orval Faubus called out the National Guard to block their path. Faubus's brazen defiance of the federal courts provoked President Eisenhower, who was no integrationist, to mobilize army troops and federalize the Arkansas National Guard in order to ensure compliance with the court. At the end of the school year, the governor closed the public schools rather than bow to demands for desegregation. Faubus's use of state power to resist integration would presage the actions of Alabama Governor George Wallace, who, several years later, would earn national attention by standing in the schoolhouse door to defend segregation at the University of Alabama.

By 1960, direct action campaigns for civil rights were building steam. On February 1, 1960, four African American students from North Carolina Agricultural and Technical College in Greensboro walked into the local Woolworth's, bought some school supplies, and sat down at the store's segregated lunch counter. This sparked a grassroots sit-in movement, led by African American students, that took aim at segregated public spaces across the South. Within two weeks of their initial action, students in eleven cities had held sit-ins, and supporters from the North as well as across the South were making plans for more. By the end of 1960, about 70,000 black students had participated in a sit-in or marched in support of the demonstrators. The sit-ins also gave birth to the Student Nonviolent Coordinating Committee (SNCC), a key organization that looked beyond the legal agenda of the older and more established NAACP.

Emmett Till, fourteen years old, murdered in Mississippi, 1955.

With a spate of unsolved bombings in the late fifties and early sixties and a city administration willing to close public facilities and withdraw services to maintain the rigid color line, Birmingham, Alabama, was known as the most repressive and rigidly segregated city in the country. In the spring of 1963, the SCLC and Martin Luther King, who was by then a national figure, launched what would be a historic campaign to bring justice to Birmingham. Thousands of African Americans marched in protest and boycotted downtown retail shops; thousands, including hundreds of children, were arrested. On May 2, Police Chief Eugene "Bull" Connor directed the arrest of more than 900 children and young adults. The next day, when the police turned dogs and fire hoses on the demonstrators, they were captured in

A roadside poster smearing Martin Luther King as a communist on the route of his three-day march from Selma to Montgomery, March 1965. President Johnson's Voting Rights Act followed.

photographs and on television, stunning the nation, and, in time, the world. Under the pressure of continuing demonstrations, the threat of intervention by federal troops, and the glare of the international spotlight, Birmingham officials repealed the city's segregation laws. In the wake of the protesters' success, mass demonstrations spread throughout the South, eventually involving more than 100,000 people. Birmingham had changed everything.

Philip A. Randolph had spearheaded the plan for a march on Washington back in 1941. In 1963, on the heels of Birmingham, he did so once more. On August 28, a quarter of a million people, of all races and from all parts of the country, gathered before the Lincoln Memorial for the historic March on Washington. The highlight of the day was Martin Luther King's speech, now known as "I Have a Dream," in which King envisioned an America free of racial prejudice. The headiness of the march evaporated when less than a month later, white terrorists bombed the Sixteenth Street Baptist Church, headquarters of the Birmingham campaign. Four young black girls preparing for Sunday school were killed. No one would be held responsible for the murders until 2002.

On July 2, 1964, African Americans won a long-sought victory when President Lyndon B. Johnson signed the Civil Rights Act into law. The Act prohibited discrimination in employment and in public facilities, and strengthened enforcement mechanisms in support of school desegregation. Another legislative victory came the next year, after voting rights campaigners were clubbed by Alabama police on what came to be known as "Bloody Sunday" during a march from Selma to Montgomery. The Voting Rights Act of 1965 instituted federal supervision of voting practices in states with a history of racial discrimination. Disenfranchisement, through such tactics as poll taxes and literacy tests, was outlawed, effectively opening the polls to southern African-American voters for the first time since the end of Reconstruction.

Civil rights protest in Memphis, 1968, past the bayonets of the National Guard.

The 1964 and 1965 acts were the death knell for Jim Crow. But discrimination and inequality were deeply entrenched in the workings of American institutions, culture, and economic practices. If legal segregation defined life's parameters for African Americans in the South, poverty and exclusion did the same for the growing ranks of blacks in northern ghettos. Just five days after President Johnson signed the Voting Rights Act, the African American neighborhood of Watts in Los Angeles erupted into nearly a week of rioting. Urban unrest broke out in other cities over the next three years. America was still, in the words of the National Committee on Civil

Disorders (known as the Kerner Commission) in 1968, "a nation moving towards two societies—one black, one white, separate and unequal."

A cartoon mocking the idea of illiterate southerners keeping blacks out of their schools on the grounds that the blacks would lower standards.

The urban uprisings of the late 1960s occasioned a shift in strategy and tactics on the part of some leaders and organizations. Martin Luther King, Jr., increasingly emphasized economic issues and human rights, supporting striking garbage workers in Memphis, protesting America's involvement in Vietnam, and developing plans for a Poor People's March on Washington. At the same time, established organizations like SNCC and groups like the Black Panther Party issued the call for "Black Power" in economics and politics, overshadowing the goal of racial integration and harmony. In place of integration, Black Power advocated independence and self-sufficiency; in place of nonviolence, Black Power advocated self-defense, by military means if necessary. The ideological rift between Civil Rights and Black Power echoed age-old tensions among African Americans on the best way to achieve liberation. Should blacks push for the United States to accept them on an equal footing with whites, or would they be better off developing their own independent institutions, communities, even their own economy? It was a question that went all the way back to slavery, and both points of view were consistently represented in each generation of African American leaders. In the 1960s, the most forceful advocate of black independence was Malcolm X. With an uncompromising stance and powerful oratory, he won many adherents among those who were impatient with the slow pace and pacifism of integration strategies. Even after his 1965 assassination, Malcolm X's ideas continued to exert a strong influence on the Black Power movement and on the younger generation.

The movement's emphasis on racial pride transformed African American cultural expression, from hairstyles to poetry. The artistic flowering of the late 1960s and 1970s gave a platform to powerful writers like Amiri Baraka (LeRoi Jones), Sonia Sanchez, and Nikki Giovanni. The Black Arts movement produced work of such volume, quality, and influence that it rivaled the Harlem Renaissance of the 1920s. The Black Power movement inspired a generation of activists who would take center stage in the fight for black political power that would emerge in America's cities in the next decades.

Montgomery bus boycott
After refusing to give up her seat to a white man in December 1955, Rosa Parks, secretary of the local chapter of the NAACP, was arrested and fingerprinted (right and above). The boycott of Montgomery's public buses continued for nearly a year until the Supreme Court ruled Alabama's bus segregation laws illegal.

Little Rock, Arkansas

In September 1957, three years after the Supreme Court had outlawed school segregation, nine African American students selected from eighty volunteers sought entry to Little Rock's still-segregated Central High School (left). They were confronted by the bayonets of the National Guard (above), which had been mobilized by Arkansas Governor Orval Faubus. As news of the confrontation spread, segregationists crowded into Little Rock in support of the governor.

High school students

White high school students crowd onto the terrace to watch events, with a few National Guardsmen among them, as the "Little Rock Nine" try to gain entry. One of the white students later said she honestly believed that if the parents had stayed away, there wouldn't have been a problem. President Eisenhower reluctantly sent federal troops and put the Arkansas National Guard under federal orders to escort the nine black students to school.

No argument
A young segregationist is seen off by the bayonets of the 327th Battle Group of the 101st Airborne, sent in to resolve the standoff at Little Rock. Governor Faubus claimed the paratroopers were "bludgeoning innocent bystanders...the warm red blood of patriotic Americans staining the cold naked unsheathed knives." In fact the only injury was to a rioter who tried to grab a soldier's rifle and got hit by its butt. The events were heavily covered by the press.

Brown's Basement Luncheonette
A sit-in by black protesters at this segregated restaurant in Oklahoma attracts the stares of inquisitive whites (above) until the police arrive to evict the protesters (right), 1958. This was one of a series of sit-ins in sixteen southern and border cities during the 1950s. But it was not until the February 1960 sit-in at Woolworth's lunch counter in Greensboro, North Carolina, that this particular form of protest took off. The sit-ins led directly to the formation of the Student Nonviolent Coordinating Committee (SNCC), which became a key spearhead of the civil rights movement.

TELEPHONE
TELEPHONE

Birmingham, Alabama

Birmingham, "the Magic City," known by blacks as "Bombingham," was the most segregated of them all. In 1963, the scene was set for one of the major confrontations of the civil rights era. Police Chief Eugene "Bull" Connor's idea of crowd control was fire hoses strong enough to knock a brick out of a wall.

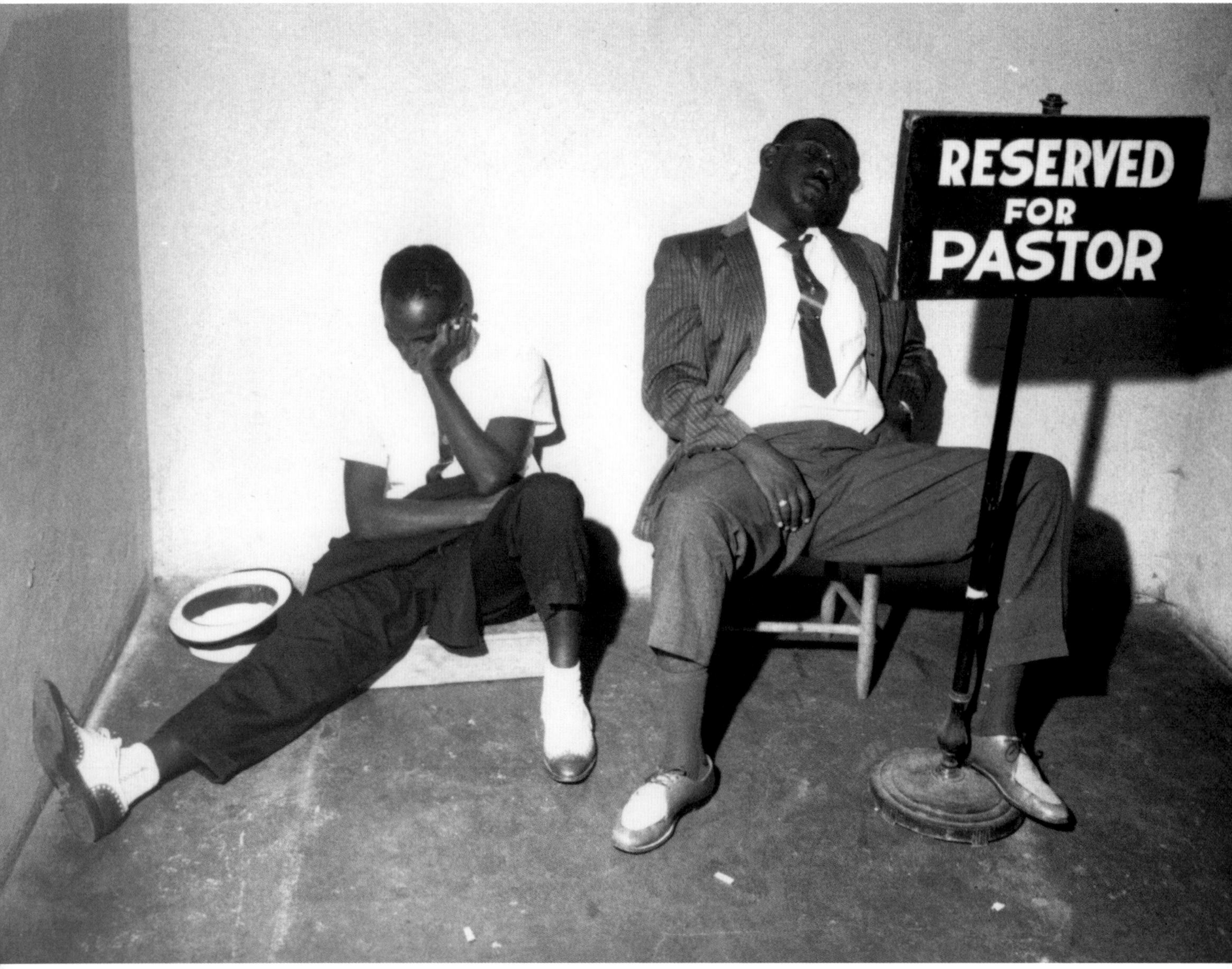

Time out
Two civil rights activists slump, exhausted, in the back room of a church during a lull in a demonstration, 1961.

Provocation
Another of "Bull" Connor's weapons of choice. The setting of police dogs and the turning of fire hoses on Birmingham protesters, when broadcast on television, had a powerful effect on the national conscience. President Kennedy said a similar picture of a dog attacking a woman made him sick.

I have a dream
Martin Luther King, Jr., addressing a crowd of nearly 250,000 before the Lincoln Memorial during the March on Washington in August 1963. In his speech, King envisioned an America free of the shackles of bigotry: "I have a dream that one day this nation will rise up and live out the true meaning of its creed: 'We hold these truths to be self-evident, that all men are created equal.'...I have a dream that my four little children will one day live in a nation where they will not be judged by the color of their skin but by the content of their character."

Selma, Alabama

The 1965 protest march from here to Montgomery was to push for the right of African Americans to register and vote. As in Birmingham, protesters met with violent reaction from local law enforcement officials. Jim Clark, Jr., the Dallas County sheriff, had already proven himself willing to imprison thousands and use electric cattle prods on high school students. Then on March 7, which became known as Bloody Sunday, marchers met with violence at the hands of Alabama state troopers on the Edmund Pettus Bridge just outside Selma in full view of television cameras. After Martin Luther King sought and received federal protection, the march went ahead with King and his wife, Coretta, at its head (above). When the protesters reached Montgomery, King spoke before the State Capitol Building (left).

OCTOBER 15. 16. 17. 18. 19. 20. 1928
PROPHET NOBLE DREW ALI FOUNDER

Black Muslims
Noble Drew Ali, with some followers in Chicago, 1928 (far left, top). Ali, who called himself a prophet of Islam, founded the Moorish Science Temple of America. His philosophy was far afield from orthodox Islam, but Ali understood the power of using Islamic symbols to define a distinct black-American identity. Elijah Muhammad (far left, below) led the Nation of Islam, a black nationalist religious organization, from 1934 until his death in 1975. He built the Nation of Islam into the wealthiest black organization of its time. A bespectacled Malcolm X in Zanzibar with a leader of the revolution there, November 1964. Among the most influential black leaders of the twentieth century, Malcolm X broke with Elijah Muhammad the same year to move toward traditional Islam and a more radical vision of human rights for African Americans. He was murdered by members of the Nation of Islam in 1965.

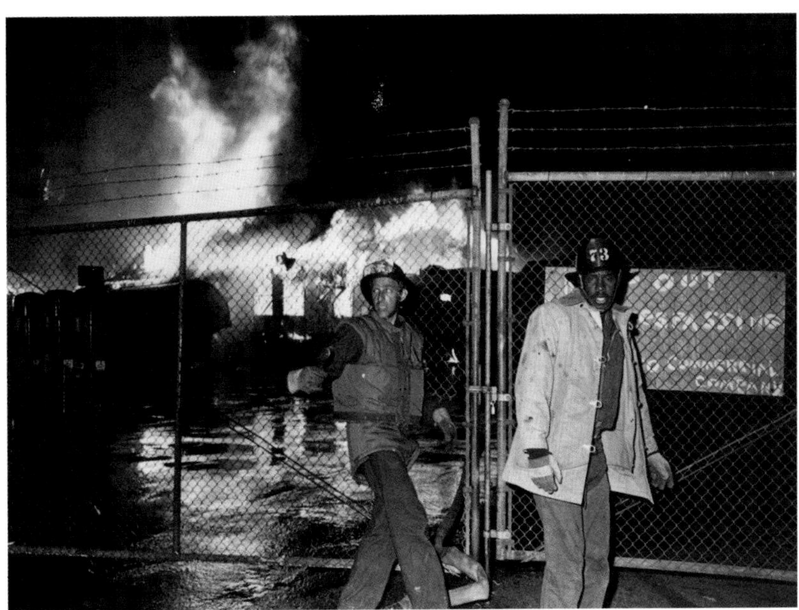

The Watts riots

On August 11, five days after the signing of the Voting Rights Act, a black neighborhood in Los Angeles exploded in violence. The trigger was police conduct during the arrest of a young driver. Over the next five days, thirty-four people died, thousands were injured, and $200 million in property was destroyed. Watts, the first in a string of disturbances in black communities nationwide, sent a clear message: Despite the dismantling of Jim Crow laws, economic and political exclusion made urban black neighborhoods highly volatile.

Freedom riders

American soldiers protect civil rights activists protesting segregation on interstate buses in 1966. Interstate terminals were finally desegregated later that year. Freedom riders had faced bombings and beatings from the beginnings of this form of protest in 1961.

LBJ and MLK
President Johnson listening to Martin Luther King discuss the importance of the Voting Rights Act in the White House, 1965. The act's passage later that year opened the polls to black voters in much of the South for the first time since Reconstruction.

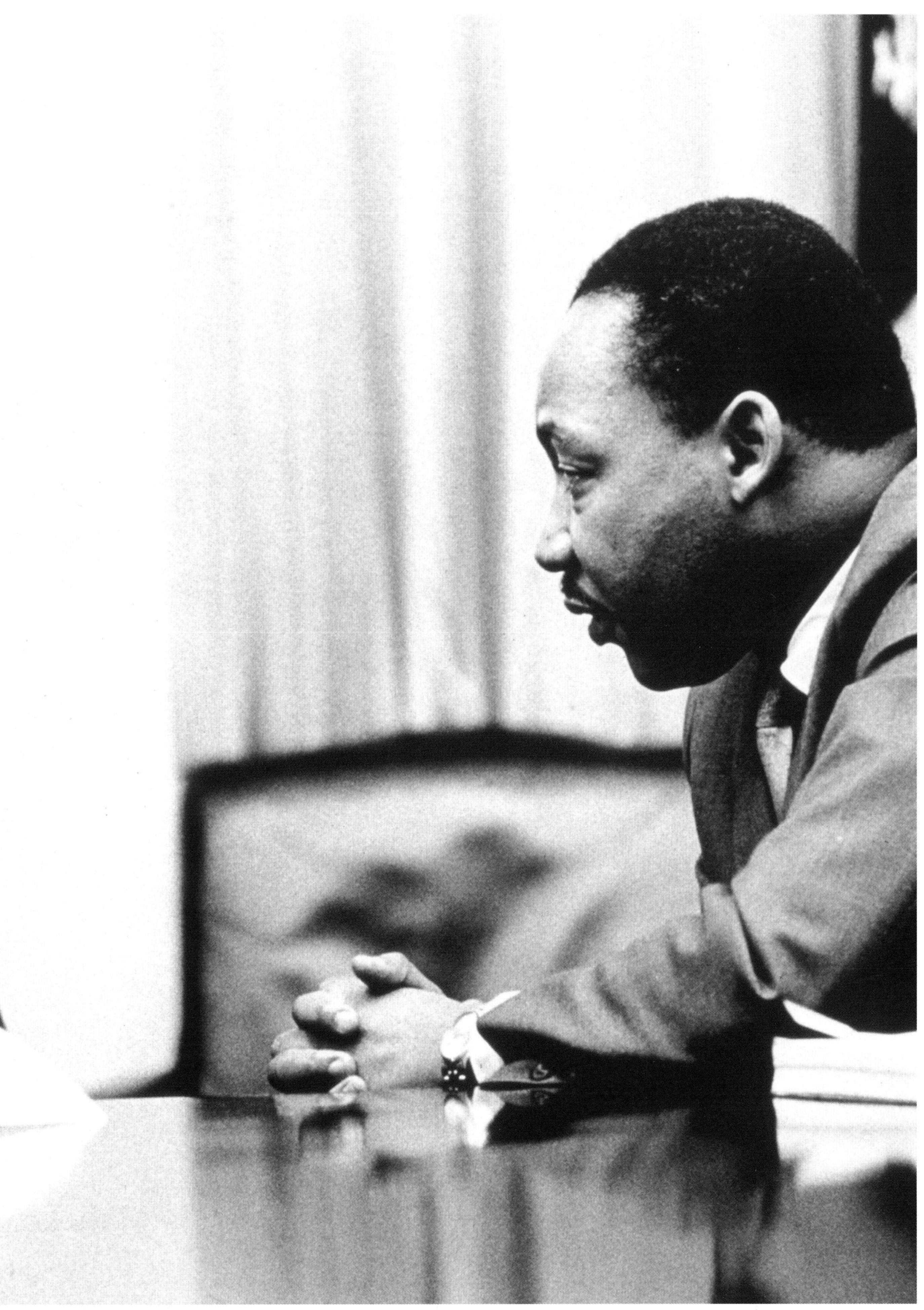

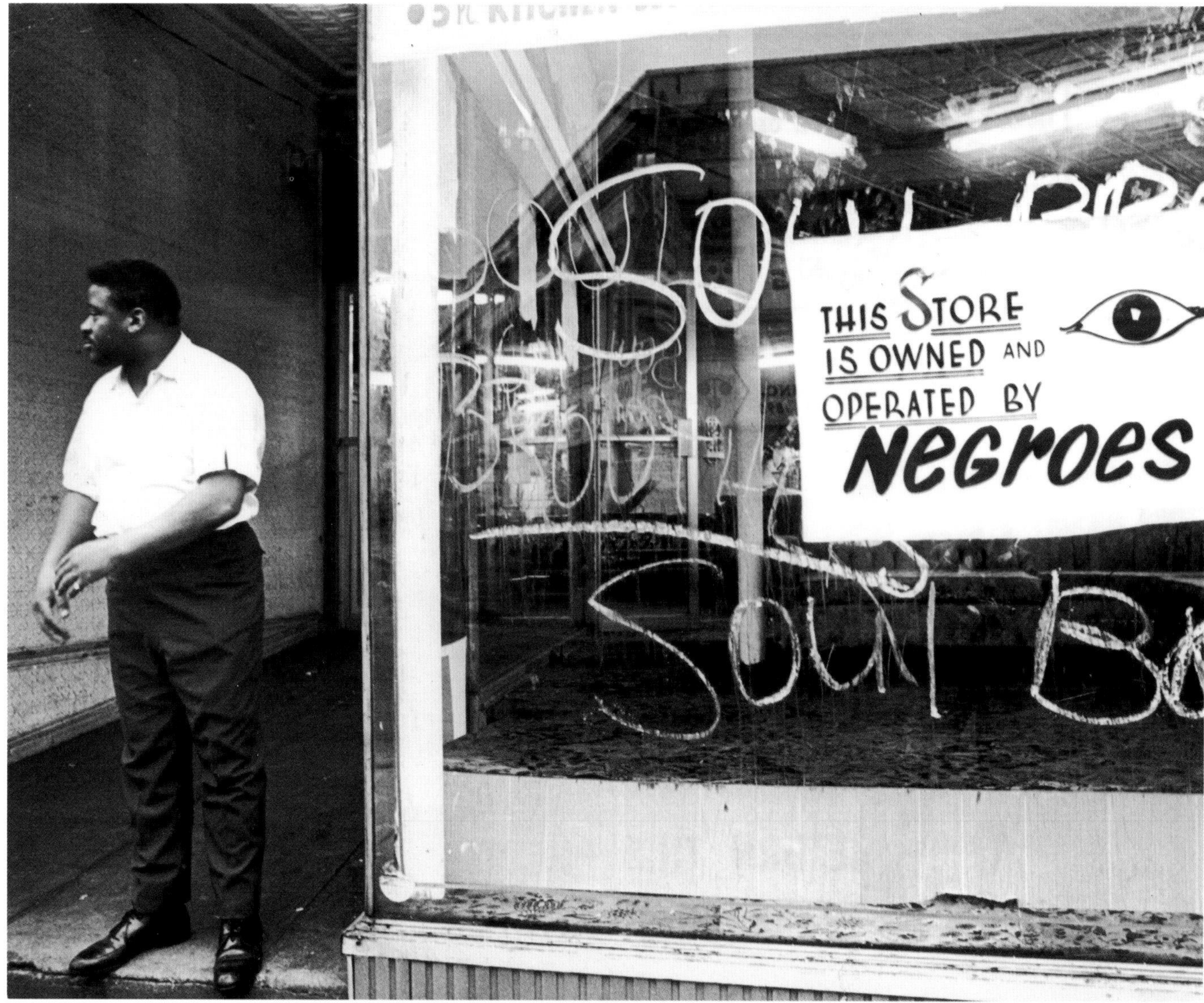

The Newark riots

An African American shopkeeper looks out anxiously from his store in New Jersey in July 1967. Knowing that in some cities black rioters spared black-owned stores, he has placed a poster and written the words "Soul Brother" on his window in an attempt to keep it from being smashed.

Protest placards
A mixed-race youth group marches in Newark to protest the use of federal troops to put down the 1967 riots there.

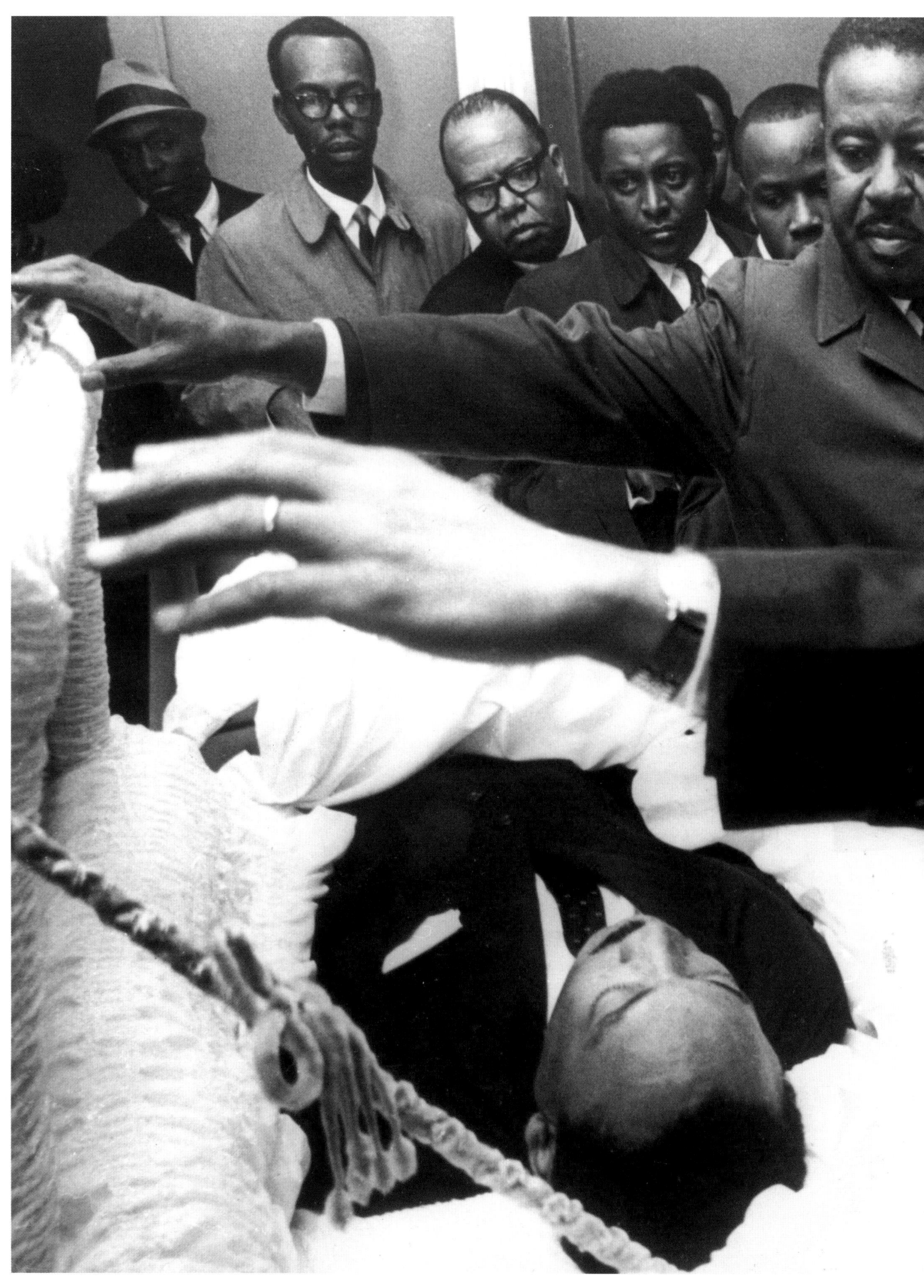

Lying in state
Colleagues pay their respects before the body of Martin Luther King in Memphis, 1968: (right to left) Andrew Young, Bernard Lee, and Ralph Abernathy. King had been assassinated on the balcony of the Lorraine Motel on April 4. News of his death resulted in worldwide shock and dismay, and prompted riots in more than one hundred U.S. cities in the following days. In 1969, James Earl Ray, an escaped white convict, pleaded guilty to King's murder. Though many investigators have suspected that Ray did not act alone, no conspiracy has ever been confirmed.

Funeral and remembrance

Mourners march behind the casket of Martin Luther King in Atlanta, Georgia, two carrying a large photograph of him (right). His parents, wife, and daughter at a memorial service for him held at Morehouse College in Atlanta (above).

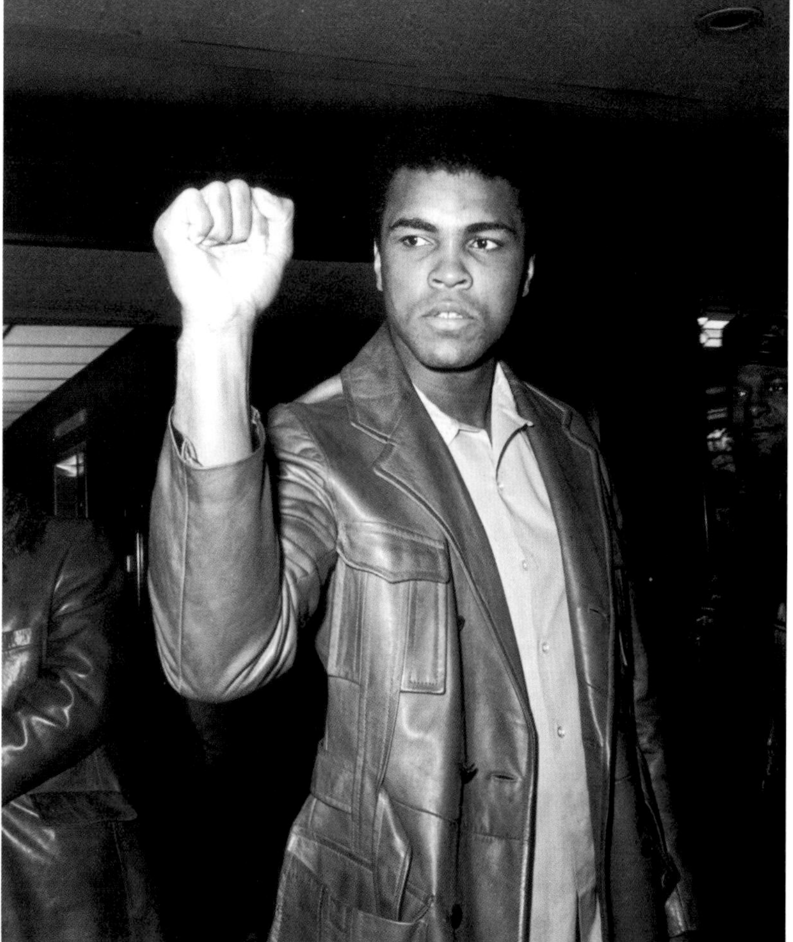

Black Power, Black Panthers

Stokely Carmichael, chairman of the SNCC in 1966, is credited with coining the term "Black Power" as a militant expression of the desire for African American self-determination. The phrase and the gesture of a clenched fist was made popular by activist athletes at the Mexico Olympics in 1968 (right): Tommy Smith (center) and Jon Carlos (right) were subsequently suspended from the U.S. team. Champion boxer Muhammad Ali raises a fist prior to a fight in 1971 (left). The Black Panther Party was founded in Oakland, California, in 1966. The Black Panthers affirmed the right of armed self-defense and quickly established themselves among young people in Oakland and in other cities nationwide. A group of Panthers in 1970 (above). It is opening day of the trial of the "Panther 21," accused of plotting to assassinate police officers and blow up buildings.

USA

Free Huey

Black Panthers in New York protest the trial of cofounder Huey Newton for the manslaughter of an Oakland policeman, 1968. FBI director J. Edgar Hoover denounced the Black Panther Party as "the greatest threat to the internal security of the country," and made the organization a target for surveillance, police raids, and covert counterintelligence operations. The Black Panthers declined as internal discord grew, and many leading members were jailed, in exile, or killed in shoot-outs with police or rival organizations. By 1980 they were no longer a political force. But community services initiated by the Black Panthers, particularly the free breakfast program for poor children and sickle-cell anemia screening, became models for government programs.

Seale and Newton

Bobby Seale and Huey Newton founded the Black Panther Party in 1966. Their initial goals were described in a ten-point platform whose demands included full employment, exemption of black men from military service, and an end to police brutality: "land, bread, housing, education, clothing, justice, and peace." The party borrowed the black panther symbol from an independent political party established the previous year by black residents of Lowndes County, Alabama. Seale won forty percent of the vote in Oakland's 1973 mayoral race, but resigned from the party the next year. Newton returned from exile to receive his Ph.D. in 1980, but was murdered in a drug-related incident in 1989.

Political women

Shirley Chisholm, who became the first black woman elected to Congress in 1968, announces her candidacy for the Democratic nomination for President in 1972 (above). While in Congress, Chisholm was a staunch advocate of black and women's rights as well as a fearless critic of President Nixon. At the behest of Governor Ronald Reagan, Angela Davis (left) was fired from her position in UCLA's philosophy department in 1969 because of her communist politics. When guns belonging to her were used in an attempt to free a Black Panther from a California courthouse, Davis was charged with kidnapping, conspiracy, and murder, though she was not near the building. She went into hiding and was placed on the FBI's ten-most-wanted list. Her arrest and subsequent imprisonment inspired "Free Angela" rallies around the world. Davis spent sixteen months in jail before being released on bail in 1972. She was later acquitted of all charges.

Misery of war
A marine weeps as he sits in a helicopter during the Vietnam War in 1968, perhaps at the memory of what he has endured or the prospect of what he might have to go through.

Bloods in Vietnam

U.S. soldiers in a dugout in Vietnam in 1968 (right). A U.S. Marine platoon sergeant looks on with satisfaction as a well, which his men have helped to construct, is put to use (above). The black casualty rate in Vietnam between 1965 and 1967 was twenty percent, nearly twice that of whites. Black soldiers referred to themselves as "bloods."

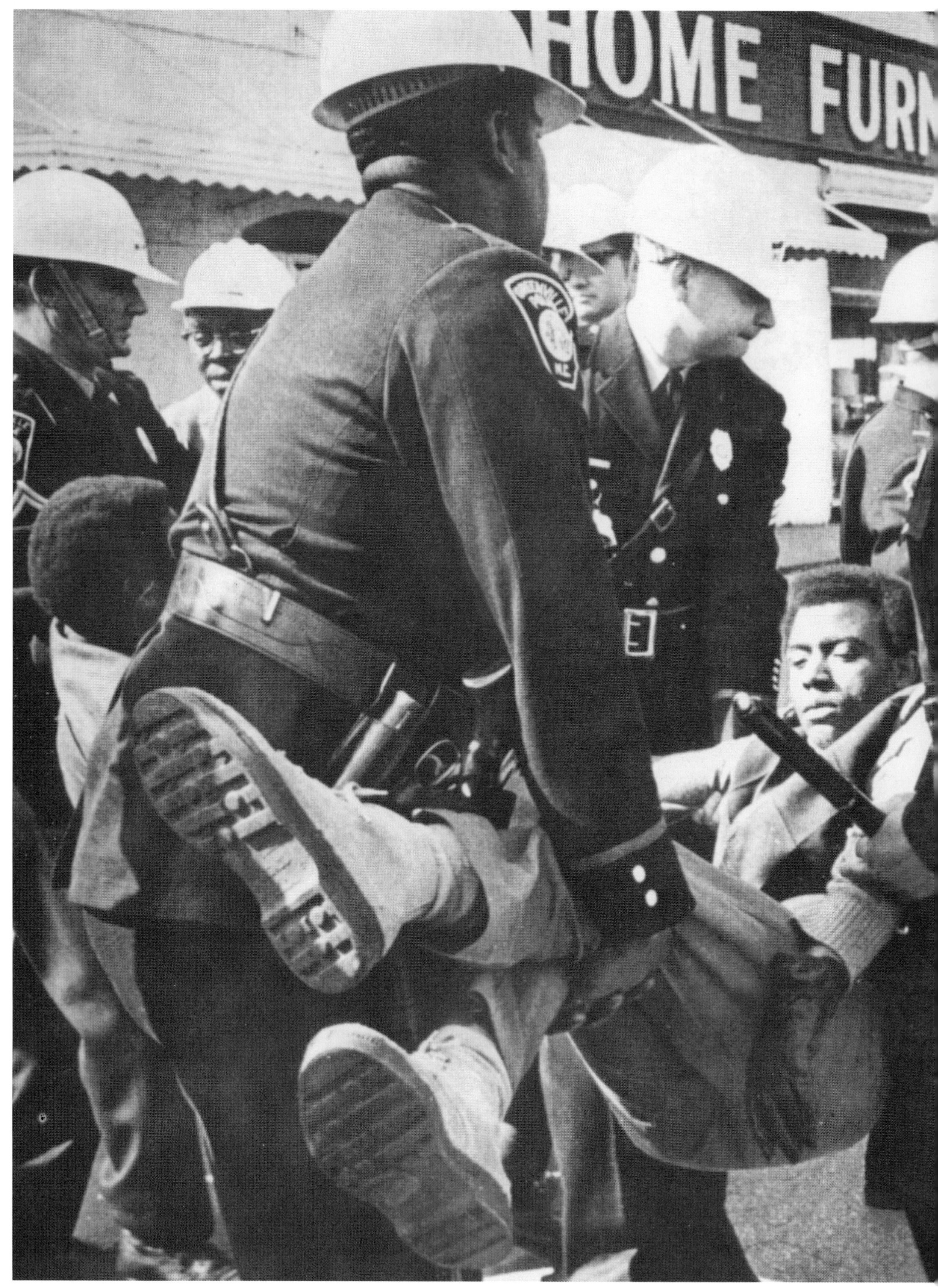
HOME FURN

The protests go on
Police carry off protesters in Greenville, North Carolina, during a march against segregated schools in February 1969.

Black Power I
Justice Thurgood Marshall, the architect of the *Brown v. Board of Education* suit and the first African American to be nominated to the Supreme Court, with President Johnson in 1967 (above); Edward Brooke, a republican from Massachusetts, the first African American to be elected to the U.S. Senate since Reconstruction (right); U.N. diplomat Ralph Bunche, the first African American to win a Nobel Peace Prize, in 1950 (far right).

Black Power II

Stokely Carmichael (far left) changed his name to Kwame Touré and lived in West Africa from 1969 until his death in 1999. Eldridge Cleaver (above) was the Black Panther Party publicist. After a 1968 shoot-out with Oakland police, he fled to Cuba, France, and Algeria with his then-wife Kathleen (left). After their 1975 return, Kathleen remained committed to radical politics, but Eldridge's views shifted toward conservative Christianity.

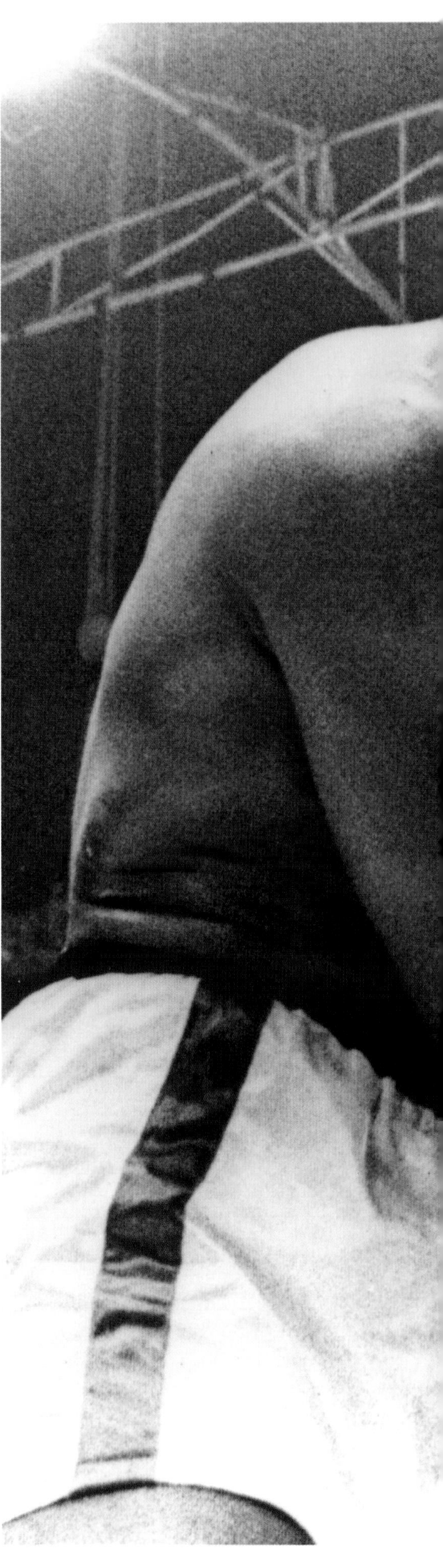

Heavyweights

Cassius Clay, shortly to become Muhammad Ali, wins his first heavyweight championship title against Sonny Liston, February 1964 (right). In 1967 his refusal to serve in the army cost him the title and landed him in prison until his sentence was reversed by the Supreme Court. Joe Frazier, at the time he defeated Ali, March 1971 (above). Ali regained the title in Kinshasa in 1974, knocking out George Foreman in the "Rumble in the Jungle." The following year Ali beat Frazier in the Philippines over fifteen rounds.

Basket and racket

Freddie "Curly" Neal and Meadowlark Lemon, two legendary members of the acrobatic basketball team the Harlem Globetrotters (above). Wilt "the Stilt" Chamberlain, winner of seven successive NBA scoring titles between 1960 and 1966 (right). Seven foot one in height, he's also known as "the Big Dipper." He once called his year with the Globetrotters the most fun of his career. Althea Gibson, the first black competitor at the U.S. Open and Wimbledon tournaments, both of which she went on to win twice between 1956 and 1958 (left).

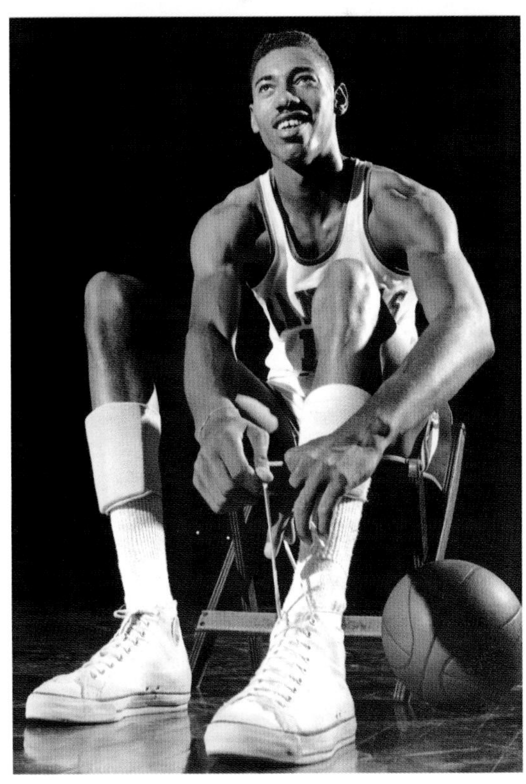

Movies

Dorothy Dandridge and Sammy Davis, Jr., on the set of *Porgy and Bess* (above left), which also starred Sidney Poitier. Poitier is seen (right) in a scene from *In the Heat of the Night* (1967), in which he starred with Rod Steiger. Director Melvin Van Peebles (below left, center) on the set of his film *Sweet Sweet-back's Baadasssss Song* (1970), which pushed at the boundaries of sex and violence on screen. Its success inspired many African Americans to get into filmmaking.

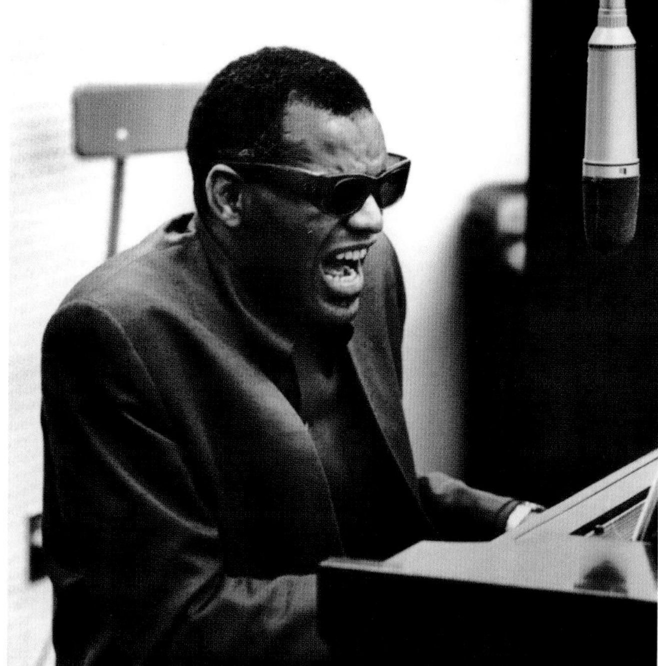

Singers, players

Ray Charles (top left), the "Father of Soul." He deepened the range of Rhythm 'n' Blues, drawing on black sacred music. Nina Simone, the "High Priestess of Soul," singing in Dallas in 1971 (top right). Singer and songwriter Stevie Wonder (bottom left), one of the jewels in the Motown crown. Thelonious Monk (bottom right), pianist and composer, one of the greatest figures in modern jazz.

Gordon Parks

A former *Life* magazine photographer renowned for his coverage of civil rights and Black Power movements, Parks (right) was the first black director of a major Hollywood movie when he made *The Learning Tree* in 1969, based on his own novel. He later directed the classic film *Shaft*.

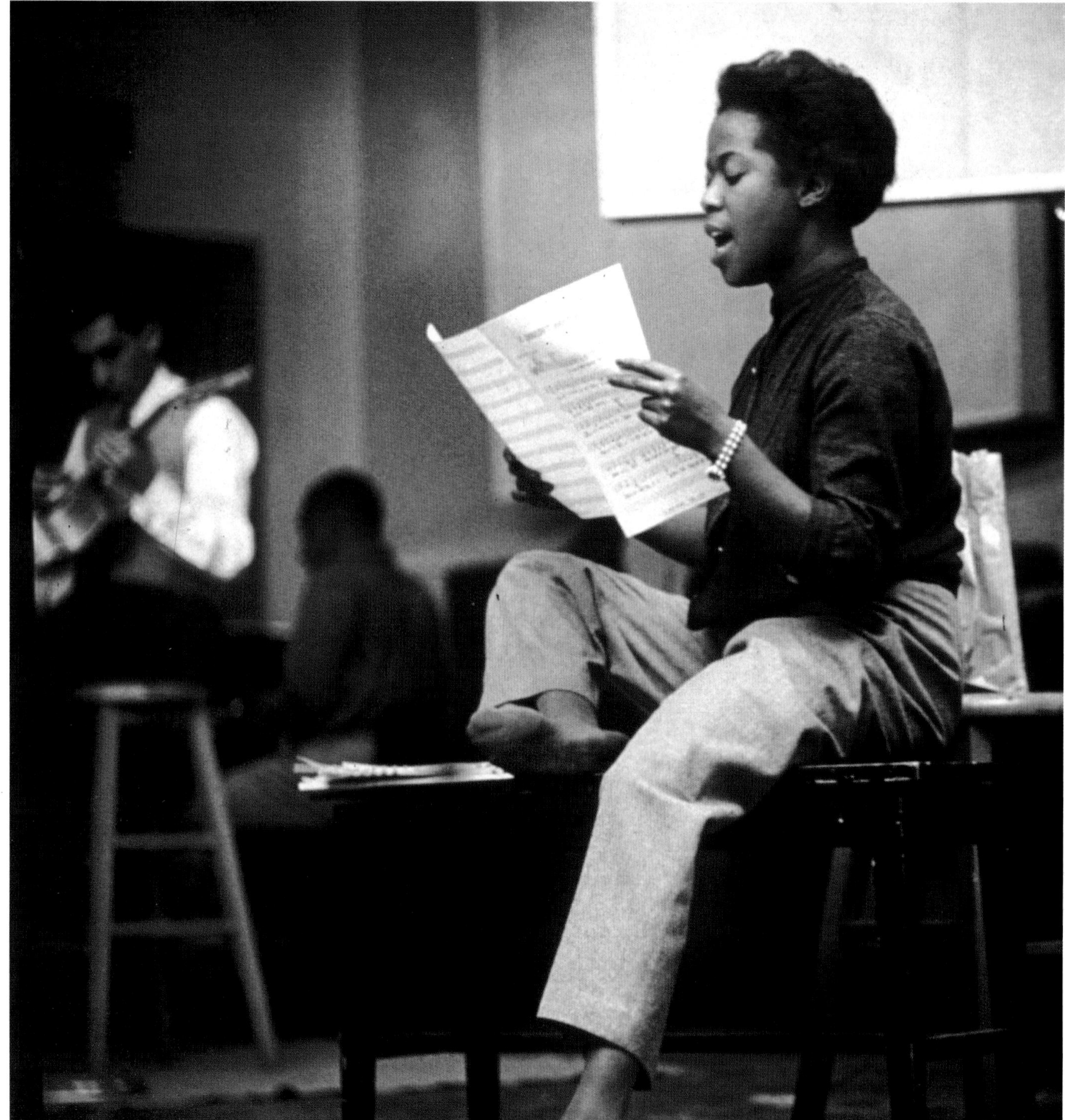

Voices

A young Sarah Vaughan, jazz singer and pianist, at a rehearsal in New York in 1950 (above). The Supremes (top left, left to right): Diana Ross, Mary Wilson, and Florence Ballard, stars of Detroit's Motown Records and the most successful female group in 1960s pop music. Dinah Washington (top right), "Queen of the Blues," in 1954. Singer Roberta Flack (bottom left). Mahalia Jackson (bottom right), "the world's greatest gospel singer."

Guitar, blues, percussion Jimi Hendrix (right) was dead of an overdose by 1970, but remains one of the most influential rock guitarists. John Lee Hooker (below left) blended country with urban blues and greatly widened the audience for the music by playing on college campuses and at music festivals. Drummer Max Roach (below right), a major influence in jazz since the 1950s.

Davis, Coltrane, Cole
The recordings of Miles Davis (left), who died in 1991, are still among the most popular in jazz history, and Davis continues to influence new generations of trumpeters. John Coltrane (below right) was the high priest of the free jazz movement of the 1960s. He remains among the most imitated and admired jazz musicians. Nat King Cole (below left) began as a jazz pianist in the 1940s but turned to pop music singing in the 1950s.

Required reading

Writer James Baldwin during the 1963 March on Washington (right). Baldwin's sharp essays gave intellectual weight to the civil rights movement and discussion about race, in particular *Notes of a Native Son*, *Nobody Knows My Name*, and *The Fire Next Time*. This last, with its argument that violence could be on the way, earned him a reputation as a prophet, though proponents of Black Power criticized the note of hope at its end. Here, Baldwin is accompanied by musicians Memphis Slim and Hazel Scott. Journalist and author Alex Haley (above). Haley, who ghostwrote *The Autobiography of Malcolm X* in 1965, traced his mother's lineage back to Africa in the mixed fiction-and-fact *Roots*. The television miniseries based on the book was among the most popular of its time.

Power of the word

Ralph Ellison (top left) published the novel *Invisible Man*, considered among the greatest of American novels, in 1952. It is but one of many tributes to its influence that Ishmael Reed (opposite) wrote a parody of it, *The Free-Lance Pallbearers*, in 1967. Lorraine Hansberry's (top right) play, *A Raisin in the Sun* (1959), was the first play by a black woman and the first directed by an African American to reach Broadway. It ran for 583 performances and was later filmed. Poet and playwright LeRoi Jones (Amiri Baraka) and writer Larry Neal (left) were major contributors to the Black Arts movement, the cultural expression of the Black Power movement. Neal edited the seminal anthology *Black Fire* in 1968.

Eight

The Contemporary Scene 1972–2002

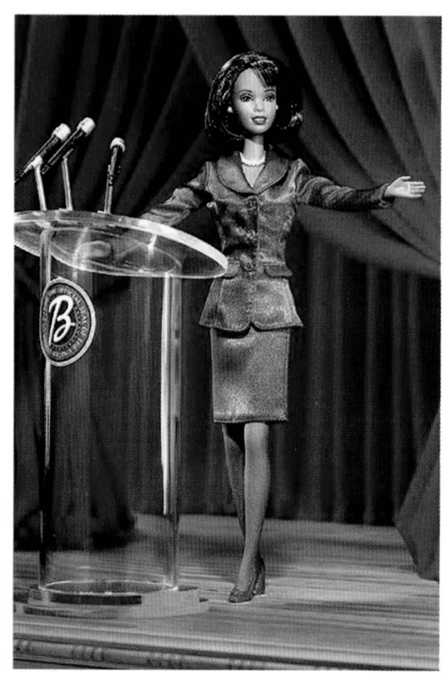

The African American President Barbie Doll, launched in 2000.

Black Americans emerged from the Civil Rights era with a sense of accomplishment tempered with apprehension. With the legal abolition of Jim Crow laws, the unfinished legal agenda of Reconstruction seemed complete; yet racial inequality remained in nearly every sphere of American life, and the economic disadvantage sustained by African Americans since the days of slavery seemed as intractable as ever. African Americans had suffered the loss of important leaders who had been considered allies: John F. Kennedy in 1963, Malcolm X in 1965, Martin Luther King, Jr., and Robert F. Kennedy in 1968, Fred Hampton in 1969. Moreover, it was revealed in 1971 that the FBI had targeted the full spectrum of black leadership, from Martin Luther King to the Black Panther Party, in a campaign of surveillance, misinformation, and disruption. Still, African Americans have managed to take advantage of the legal advances of the Civil Rights era to make significant strides in politics, business, and culture.

In the 1980s and 1990s, African Americans pushed forward the gains of the 1965 Voting Rights Act by electing black officials to office in record numbers. There were lingering issues of fairness in voter registration, districting, and other voting rights issues, but in southern cities and towns, as well as the northern urban areas where they had long enjoyed the franchise, black voters elected school board officials, state legislators, and local executives. Black mayors came to power in major cities such as New York, Chicago, Detroit, Philadelphia, and for twenty years starting in 1973, Los Angeles. In most cases, however, black big-city mayors inherited dwindling coffers, crumbling infrastructures, and rising expectations from both needy black constituencies and largely white business communities.

Previous page
Secretary of State Colin Powell takes a question at a news conference at the State Department in April 2002.

At the national level, Jesse Jackson's credible runs for the presidency in 1984 and 1988, and the 1991 confirmation hearings of Supreme Court Justice Clarence Thomas put black Americans squarely in the spotlight. The Congressional Black Caucus (CBC), which has grown from thirteen in 1971 to thirty-eight in 2000, has become known as the most reliably progressive group of congressional representatives. And growing numbers of African Americans have been appointed to key positions in the federal government. President Bill Clinton, upon taking office in 1993, appointed a record five black cabinet members. President George W. Bush was the first to appoint African Americans in major foreign policy positions: Colin Powell as Secretary of State and Condoleezza Rice as National Security Advisor. To be sure, questions remain about whether visible black appointees, particularly those as conservative as Powell and Rice, improve the lives of a still disadvantaged black population. But the fact that African Americans would generally have been barred from such positions as recently as a generation ago is undeniable.

The new state flag of Georgia, incorporating the old Confederate flag, flying in January 2002, seen as a provocation by African Americans.

The racial terrain in the business arena has changed as well. Prior to the 1980s, black-owned businesses had largely been built by serving black consumers. Taking advantage of the failure of the mainstream business sector to serve the African American market, some black businesspeople were able to make a fortune through such companies as Soft Sheen and Johnson Products in hair care and cosmetics, *Jet* and *Ebony* in publishing, and the influential Motown in the recording industry. More recently, however, the mainstream business community has begun to recognize the value of the African American market and has bought out a number of black-owned companies, including Johnson Products, Motown, and Black Entertainment Television (BET). At the same time, more black executives have made inroads into corporate America, and a handful sit at the very top as CEOs: Kenneth Chenault at American Express, Richard Parsons at entertainment giant AOL-Time Warner, Franklin Raines at the Fortune 100 mortgage company Fannie Mae, and the late Reginald Lewis, who before his death in 1993 had amassed a billion-dollar business through the acquisition of TLC Beatrice International.

Mae Jemison (right), the first African American woman in space, aboard the Space Shuttle *Endeavour* in 1992.

In music, the longstanding dominance of African-American cultural expression has expanded in the modern era. In particular, the influence of hip-hop, encompassing music, language, movies, and clothing, has spread far beyond the African American community to embrace white suburban youth and countries from Brazil to Indonesia. A handful of the hip-hop leaders of the 1980s and 1990s, including Russell Simmons and Sean "P.

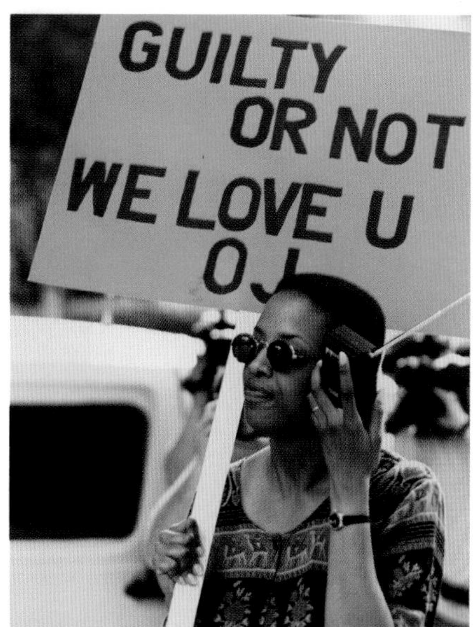

An O. J. Simpson supporter listens to his preliminary hearing on her radio outside the Los Angeles Criminal Court, 1994. He was later acquitted of the murder of his ex-wife and her friend, Ron Goldman.

Diddy" Combs, have leveraged hip-hop record sales to create larger and more complex business enterprises. Hip-hop is not the only form of black music to thrive in the contemporary age. Jazz, a mainstay of American culture since the 1920s, has enjoyed a renaissance since the 1980s, with trends toward innovation by such artists as saxophonist Henry Threadgill and vocalist Cassandra Wilson, as well as institutionalization by the likes of trumpeter Wynton Marsalis, Director of Jazz at Lincoln Center. In opera, several African American artists are among those at the very top of the field.

Civil rights organizations continue to criticize the television and motion picture industries for stereotypical portrayals of African Americans, as well as for the dearth of blacks in positions of power. But there are some notable exceptions. In television, both actor/comedian Bill Cosby and talk show host Oprah Winfrey (who was by 1998 the wealthiest black person in the U.S.) acquired the lucrative distribution rights to their own shows and used the profits to expand their business and philanthropic activities. In the motion picture industry, Spike Lee has, since the 1980s, made profitable films with black stories and actors, and has in the process inspired and trained a generation of young filmmakers. In the theater, African Americans George Wolfe, Artistic Director of the prestigious Joseph Papp Public Theater, and Pulitzer Prize–winning playwrights August Wilson and Suzan-Lori Parks have broken new ground by insisting that black stories and perspectives belong in the mainstream of American culture.

Since the 1970s, the world of sports has become progressively more dominated by black athletes and the salaries of those at the top have reached staggering proportions. But in sports, from basketball to golf, from baseball to tennis, professional athletes receive a growing share of their income from lucrative commercial endorsements. A star runner sporting a logo on his shoes or a celebrity tennis player wearing a brand name on her visor is worth money to both advertisers and athletes. Widespread campaigns against the use of sweatshop labor by some athletic shoe manufacturers has done nothing to dampen the willingness of celebrity athletes to don logos in the name of a good contract. Commercialized representations of contemporary athletes are a stark contrast to the militant images of athletes from the Black Power period. Many of today's black athletes contribute to community projects in their hometowns or lend their names to charitable activities, but most steer clear of taking political stands that might compromise their market value.

A 1972 film poster. The plot summary: Interior decorators buy the coffin of an African prince bitten by Dracula.

Despite the clear achievements of African Americans in recent years, the majority of blacks still languish near the bottom of the nation's economic and social hierarchy. On nearly every indicator of socioeconomic status, from employment and educational attainment to health and home ownership, African Americans lag behind whites, and in some cases, behind other minority groups. Overt discrimination remains completely unchecked in some instances, as recent studies on mortgage lending and criminal sentencing show. But more pernicious are the structural inequities built into nominally color-blind institutions. "White flight" combines with the policy of funding education through real estate taxes to yield great discrepancies in the quality of education between impoverished city schools and affluent suburban ones. Historic relegation of African Americans to low-paid service sector jobs makes them more vulnerable to a downturn in the economy. In the first years of the twenty-first century, more African-American men are ensnared in the criminal justice system than are in college.

The Commodores, a successful pop group of the late 1970s, fronted by Lionel Richie (on the right in the middle row), help to sell some beer.

Redressing persistent racism is made more difficult by a steady reversal of affirmative action policies. Beginning with the *Bakke* decision in 1978, the Supreme Court outlawed the use of quotas in higher education, local set-asides for minority contractors, and efforts to increase the number of black-owned television and radio stations. Affirmative action has also been narrowed or, as in the case of higher education in California, eliminated by executive action and by referendum.

As has happened in the past, black frustration over continuing inequities and unfair treatment at the hands of the police has on occasion boiled over. Civil unrest in Miami in 1980, Los Angeles in 1992, and Cincinnati in 2001 are grim and startling reminders of the alienation of many African Americans from the dominant discourse of success. White hostility may be couched in the code words of modern politicians or as overt as the revival of the Confederate flag by southern state governments in the 1990s. In either case it is clear that in some quarters, powerful resentment toward African Americans remains.

With elimination of legal segregation and with the high visibility of African Americans in popular culture, the way to progress for the majority of black Americans in the twenty-first century has become a trickier path. But the future story of black America, like its past, will be the continuing struggle to make America true to its democratic ideals.

Black is beautiful

Contestants for the Miss Black America title line up in 1972. Significantly, only two non-Afro coiffures are visible.

BLACK
MISS BLACK MASSACHUSETTS
MISS BLACK MINNESOTA
MISS BLACK MISSOURI
MISS BLACK NEW JERSEY

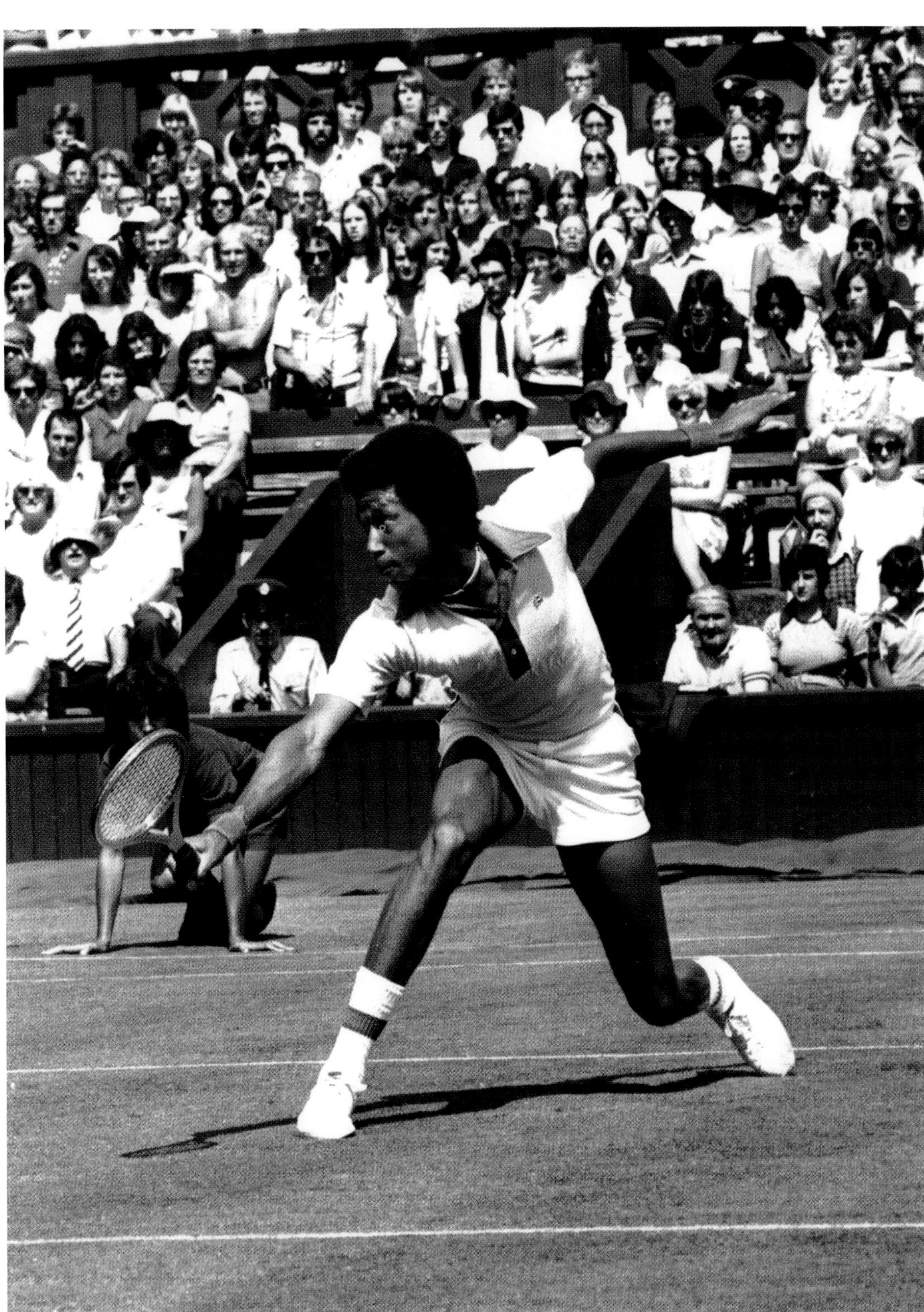

Big strides
Arthur Ashe (above) winning his Wimbledon singles title in 1975, the year he was ranked number one in the world. A heart condition forced his retirement in 1980 and he died in 1993 of AIDS. Ed Moses (left) winning the men's 400 meter hurdles at the 1984 Olympics in Los Angeles.

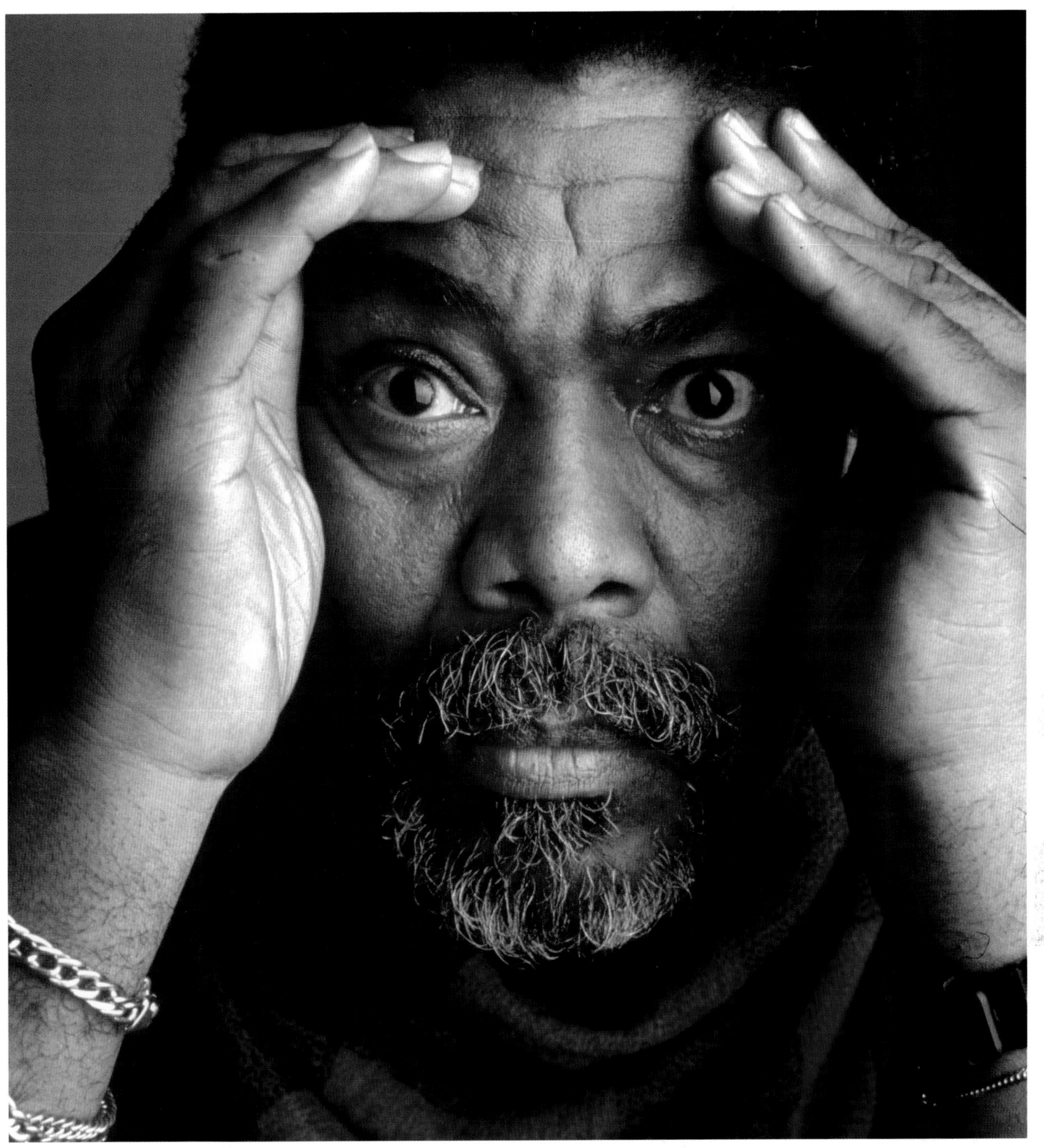

Alvin Ailey
The dancer, choreographer, and founder of the Alvin Ailey Dance Theater, pictured in 1988, the year before his death (above). The unique style of the AAADT, founded in 1958, is beloved around the world, forging a new strand of uniquely African American modern dance. It also performs other modern classics. A group of Alvin Ailey dancers in 1974 (left).

Divas

Three world-class opera singers: Jessye Norman in Berlioz's *The Trojans* at the Met in New York (above), Shirley Verrett (left), and Leontyne Price in *Aida*, her farewell performance at the Met in 1984 (far left).

Rap

"It's like a jungle sometimes." Pioneering rapper Grandmaster Flash (right) and his Bronx-based group the Furious Five were the premier DJ-rap team of the early 1980s. These words, taken from his rap *The Message*, introduced rap's preoccupations: urban fear and loathing. Chuck D (fist clenched) and Flavor Flav (front, center) of Public Enemy at the Apollo, Manchester, England, 1989 (left).

PH-490
FISHER
STEREO
FULL AUTO STOP

Pop

Marsha Hunt, more popular in the U.K. than her native U.S. (above top). Tina Turner in Versace at the Kremlin in Moscow in 1996 (left). Michael Jackson in Brazil in 1993 (right). His 1982 album *Thriller* was the best-selling pop album of all time, selling over forty million copies.

Trumpet, blues, soul

Trumpet virtuoso Wynton Marsalis (above) performing at a downtown Manhattan store in November 2001 to show support for victims and their families after September 11. He is equally at home with jazz and classical music. Soul singer Marvin Gaye (top left) and funk-soul pioneer James Brown: "Mr. Dynamite," "the Hardest Working Man in Show Business," and "the Godfather of Soul" (top right). B. B. King, the blues master (bottom left), and Dionne Warwick, whose renditions of Burt Bacharach and Hal David compositions were part of the soundtrack of the 1960s and 1970s (bottom right).

Jets vs. Seahawks
New York Jets' Aaron Glenn intercepts a pass intended for Joey Galloway of the Seattle Seahawks in 1998. Although sixty-seven percent of all players in the NFL are black, there are no African-American owners and only a few managers and coaches.

JETS
31

Seoul Olympics 1988

Carl Lewis (left) in the 100 meter race. He won after Canadian Ben Johnson tested positive for drugs. Lewis won ten Olympic gold medals between 1984 and 1996, including four medals for the long jump. Florence Griffith-Joyner's three golds and a silver gained at Seoul (above). Her gold medals were for the 100, 200, and 4 x 100 meter relay.

USA
TDK
1357
GÖTEBORG '95
935

USA
TDK
USA
GÖTEBORG '95

Sporting prowess
The U.S. women's Olympic basketball team celebrates gold at Atlanta, 1996 (left). Michael Johnson after winning the 200 meters at the Gothenburg World Championships, 1995 (middle left). Shaquille O'Neal scores as the U.S. defeats Brazil in 1994 (far left). Jackie Joyner-Kersee doing the high jump, 1994 (below). Gail Devers celebrates after winning the 100 meters at the Atlanta Olympics, 1996 (below center). Butch Reynolds in the 4 x 400 meter relay at Gothenburg, 1995 (below, far left).

Concentration and elation

Tiger Woods lines up a putt on his way to win the Masters in 2002 (top left). Chainey Umphrey on the rings at the Atlanta Olympics, 1996 (above). Venus Williams, elated after beating Martina Hingis in the semifinals at Wimbledon, 2000 (left). She went on to win the final. Michael Johnson's golden shoes, with their trademarked logo, prepare to leave the blocks at the Sydney Olympics in 2000 (far left).

Authors

The novelist and Pulitzer and Nobel prizewinner Toni Morrison (above). Among her acclaimed books are *Song of Solomon*, *Tar Baby*, and *Beloved*. Maya Angelou (next page, top right), the first volume of whose autobiography, *I Know Why the Caged Bird Sings*, brought her fame in 1970. She has also distinguished herself as a poet and actress. Harvard professor and prominent intellectual Henry Lewis Gates (next page, left), editor, most recently, of *The Bondwoman's Narrative*, a novel by escaped slave Hannah Crofts that he discovered in 2001. Alice Walker (next page, center), novelist, poet, teacher, essayist, political activist, and most famous for her 1983 novel *The Color Purple*. Cornel West (next page, right), philosopher, activist, and theologian, Princeton University professor.

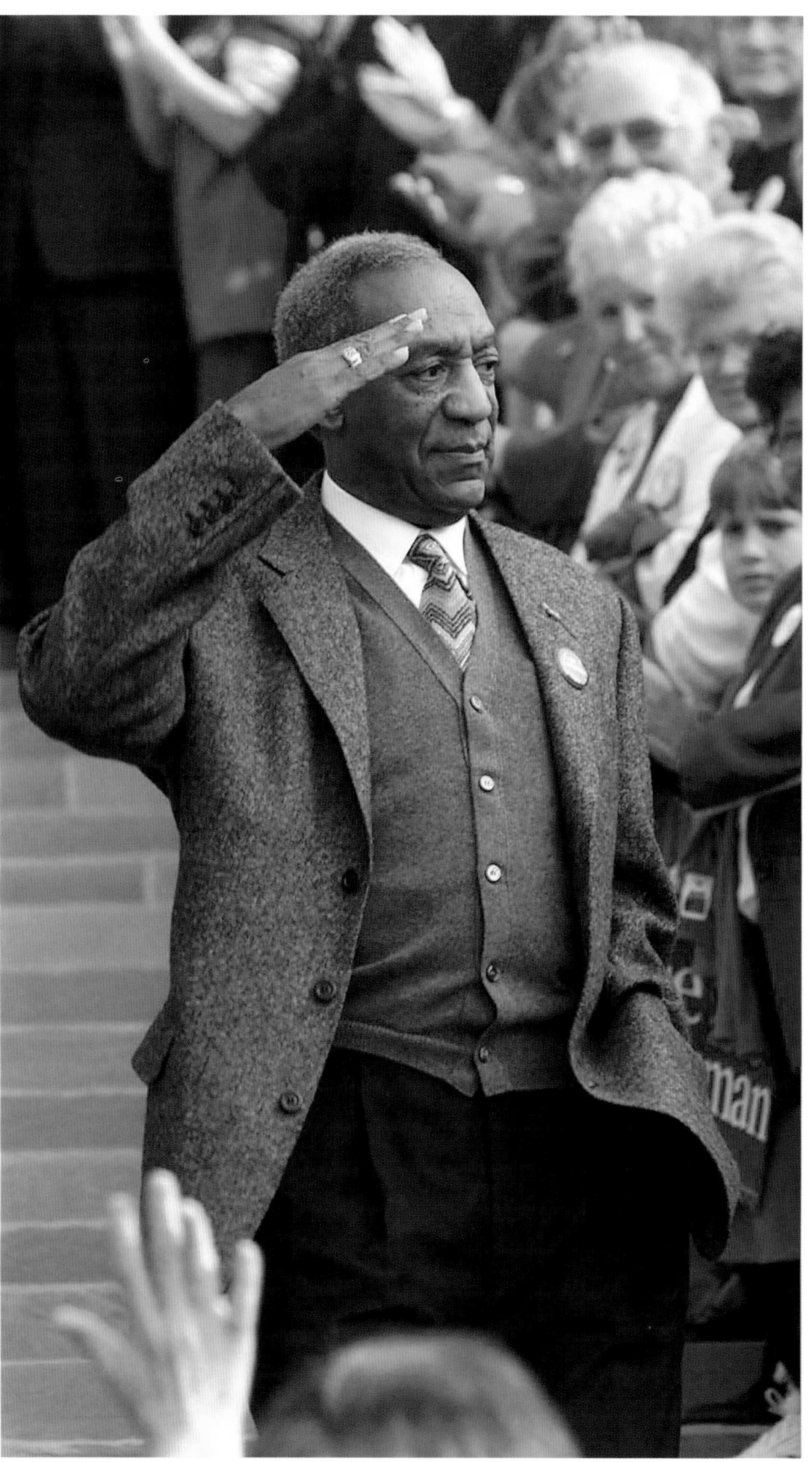

Bill Cosby
He was the first black person to star in a predominantly white TV series, *I Spy*, in the 1960s. *The Cosby Show*, which ran from 1984 to 1992, made a point of undermining racial stereotypes by portraying an upper-middle-class black family. Cosby has been heavily involved in philanthropy, and in 1989 he and his wife gave $20 million to Spelman College. Here he emerges after speaking at a Democratic campaign rally in 2000.

Oprah Winfrey
Her talk show, the most popular in history, began as *A.M. Chicago* and was first syndicated in 1986. By 1997, fifteen to twenty million viewers were watching it each day, and it was broadcast in 132 countries. Here she hams it up for the camera at *Vanity Fair*'s post-Oscars party in 2002.

Music and protest
Tupac Shakur, "Shining Spirit, thankful to God," a.k.a. MC New York (left). Among the most influential of young rappers and poets in the 1990s, Shakur lived a life of intense creativity and danger. Criticized for glorifying what he called the "thug life," Shakur's lyrics addressed the challenges of being young, black, and poor, and often foreshadowed his own violent death. His murder in 1996 at the age of twenty-five continues to inspire artistic work and scholarly critique. His most successful CD, *Until the End of Time*, was released after his death. Prince (right), at a live gig. The word "SLAVE" is inscribed on his cheek in protest against the terms extracted from him, and other artists, by recording companies. The issue of performers' rights and freedom, particularly for black artists, resurfaced in the 1990s.

Run-D.M.C.

The "fat-lace, adidas-sporting" rappers Run-D.M.C. (right), belting it out in concert. Many critics consider hip-hop to be the greatest contemporary African-American art form. While many of the most popular and innovative hip-hop artists have continued the tradition of black protest in music, others have been criticized for romanticizing and legitimizing violence and misogyny.

A posse of rappers (clockwise from left) Destiny's Child, a girl group from Houston, Texas, who won the NAACP Image Award for *The Writing's on the Wall.* Sean "P. Diddy" Combs taking part in LIFEbeat's UrbanAID 2 concert in New York City, April 9, 2002, to increase awareness of HIV prevention programs. Two awards for hip-hop star Missy Elliott at the 44th Annual Grammy Awards, Los Angeles, February 27, 2002. Lil' Kim, a brash, explicitly sexual, and controversial rapper, whose career was launched with *Hard Core* in 1996.

Hollywood heroes
Five actors whose success points to a measure of greater access to a wider range of roles for black Americans in Hollywood: (clockwise from above) Will Smith, star of *Ali* and *Men in Black*; Halle Berry and Denzel Washington with the highest honors in acting they received at the 2002 Academy Awards for, respectively, *Monster's Ball* and *Training Day*; Whoopi Goldberg; and Samuel L. Jackson arriving at Paramount Studios for the premiere of *Changing Lanes*.

abc

Bamboozled

Savion Glover and Jada Pinkett Smith (above) in a scene from Spike Lee's 2001 film *Bamboozled*, a satirical look at the trials and tribulations of black writers in Hollywood. In the film, a ratings-hungry network executive backs a comedy about two shuffling black men who live in a watermelon patch in the Deep South—"a real coon show," as the executive puts it. More than any other black director, Lee has been able to garner the power in Hollywood to continue to make films that challenge conventional stereotypes.

Writers and directors
(Clockwise from far right) The playwright Suzan-Lori Parks, winner of the 2002 Pulitzer Drama Prize for her play *Topdog/Underdog*. Director Spike Lee in Beverly Hills for the premiere of his film *Jim Brown, All American*, April 2002. Playwright and Artistic Director of the Joseph Papp Public Theater George C. Wolfe. Director Kasi Lemmons, who won critical acclaim for her films *Eve's Bayou* and *Caveman's Valentine*.

Facing the old enemy

Darrell Nichols, president of the northwest Ohio NAACP, stares in dismay at a rally of the Ku Klux Klan in Defiance, Ohio, March 20, 1999 (right). Nichols, who was amazed that in 1999 the KKK still existed on his doorstep, later reported that the rally "brought tears to my eyes." Though the 1990s saw another of the KKK's repeated attempts to reassert itself in the old mold (above), more contemporary Klansmen have, like Louisiana state official David Duke, recast themselves in the role of legitimate politicians.

NAACP

Political wing

Activist and clergyman Jesse Jackson with ANC leader Oliver Tambo and antiapartheid campaigner Bishop Trevor Huddleston (left). Jackson's campaigns for the Democratic nomination for President in 1984 and 1988 broke ground in progressive multiracial electoral politics. Former mayor of New York David Dinkins speaking on the anniversary of Martin Luther King's birthday in January 2002. Tom Bradley (above), the first black mayor of Los Angeles, at a press conference in April 1993. Bradley held office for twenty years.

Policing the world

Under the watchful, if bemused, eyes of a local couple, an African American soldier patrols a town in Bosnia, January 1996 (right). PFC Daryl Robinson shares his lunch with Abdullaha, a local Afghan working on the United States air base at Kandahar, February 2002.

In the Oval Office

Secretary of State Colin Powell receives a pat of approval from National Security Advisor Condoleezza Rice at the White House, May 2002 (above). The occasion was the meeting between President George W. Bush and Israeli Prime Minister Ariel Sharon.

Speaking out

(Clockwise from top) Elaine R. Jones, Director-Counsel of the NAACP Legal Defense and Educational Fund. She is the first woman to stand in the shoes of Thurgood Marshall. Illinois Democrat Senator Carol Moseley-Braun, the first African-American woman to serve in the Senate, campaigning on behalf of an investigation into "search and seizure" procedures, July 1998. Anita Hill, professor of law, Brandeis University, at a press conference in Washington D.C. Hill's accusations of sexual harassment nearly derailed the Supreme Court nomination of Clarence Thomas. California Congresswoman Maxine Waters questions a witness at a meeting of the U.S. House of Representatives Judiciary Committee, December 1998.

After the riot

In the aftermath of rioting in downtown Cincinnati, two black men await their fate for breaking the curfew laws, April 14, 2001. The riots flared after a white police officer shot and killed nineteen-year-old Timothy Thomas. Thomas was the fifteenth young black man to be shot by Cincinnati police in five years.

Al Sharpton

Reverend Al Sharpton (above) speaking at a press conference in Miami, Florida, where he condemned the sexual assault by NYPD officers on Abner Louima, standing beside him, March 7, 2002. Women gather outside the United Nations building in New York City, February 2000, to protest against the acquittal of four white police officers charged with shooting Amadou Diallo forty-one times.

Millions on the march

Part of the vast crowd that gathered for the Million Woman March on the Benjamin Franklin Parkway, Philadelphia, October 25, 1997 (above). The march was aimed to increase solidarity among African American women. Louis Farrakhan (right), leader of the Nation of Islam, addresses tens of thousands of supporters who participated in the Million Family March down the National Mall, Washington D.C., October 16, 2000. Both events were modeled on the 1995 Million Man March, organized by a coalition led by Farrakhan.

FAMILY
MILLION
MARCH
2000

Leaping for the heights
Hakeem Olajuwon of the Houston Rockets and Shaquille O'Neal of the Orlando Magic struggle for supremacy on the basketball court, Houston, 1995. The continued success of African Americans in basketball, boxing, football, tennis, and almost all American sports has yet to be mirrored in the control and administration of sports generally.

SPALDING

Editor's note

Compiling a book like this is a huge effort. The archives of Getty Images provided wealth and inspiration, but it would have been a very different book without the contributions of other archives and their curators and archivists who provided so much knowledge, advice, and time. With special thanks to: James Huffman at the Schomburg Center; Stephen Jones at the Beinecke Library; Coi Drummond-Gehrig of the Denver Public Library; Jan Lovell of the *Detroit News*; Maggie Mayo and Laura Wurzal of the Press Assocciation; Teresa Roane at the Valentine Richmond History Center; Gary Franklin; of course our own Valerie Zars, Blossom Lefcourt, Peter Rohowsky, and Kristeen Ballard of Getty Images in New York; and Laura Wyss who sought out images in New York and Washington. We would also like to thank Professor Peter Fraser, Wyn Thomas of Ffilmiau Tawe, and Professor David Killingray.

An extra special thanks goes to Joëlle Ferly, who drove the research with able assistance from Jennifer Jeffrey; to Michael Rand, whose patience and brilliant editor's eye carried the project through many a long day; to Mick Hodson, who actually put together the book; to Sam Hudson, who shined and sharpened the text; and in a class of her own, our author, Marcia A. Smith, who took on this project at short notice and brought to it her great knowledge and an imperturbable flair and style.

CBM

(Previous page) Photographer Ernst Haas captured the spirit of Mardi Gras, 1979. (Above) Author Richard Wright focusing on his subject in Chicago in the mid-1940s.

Picture Sources

Getty Images

Hulton Archive

Erich Auerbach 332 bottom right
Alan Band Photos 327
CBS Photo Archive 352
Harry Benson 306
Deborah Feingold 353
Chris Felver 369 bottom right
Terry Fincher 321
Frances Benjamin Johnston Collection 122
Bruce Davidson 302–3
Jack Delano 201, 212, 244
Frank Driggs Collection 126, 127, 170–1, 172 left, 172 right, 173, 176, 335 top left, 337 bottom right
George Eastman House 54, 74–5; Samuel N. Fox 36 top; Alexander Gardner 47; Lewis W. Hine 136–7, 140–1, 157, 160, 161, 169, 190, 228–9; J. E. McClees 55; Nickolas Muray 166 top; William M. Vander Weyde 134, 135; A. D. White 68
Walker Evans 185, 221
Alexander Gardner 42 right
Bernard Gotfryd 340 top left, 355 top
Ernst Haas 394–5
O. Pierre Havens 99
Shel Hershorn UT Austin 288, 289
Tad Hershorn 332 top right
Historic Photo Archive 128
David Knox 50
Lambert 261
Dorothea Lange 208–9, 213
Russell Lee 211, 224–5
Herman Leonard 269, 275, 334
John Margolies Collection 168, 220, 262
Doug McKenzie 359 middle left
Metronome 271 left
Museum of the City of New York: Berenice Abbott 184, 216–17; Byron Collection 121, 141 bottom
Matthew Brady 72–73
New York Times Co. 231, 310; Don Hogan Charles 317; Sara Krulwich 354; Ernest Sisto 266
The Observer/Chris Smith 326
J. A. Palmer 98
Bob Parent 268, 270 right, 274, 335 top right, 336 bottom right
Gordon Parks 249
Roz Payne 312 top, 325 bottom right
Charles Peterson 177, 189
Popperfoto 367 bottom
Anthony Potter Collection 245 bottom, 252 bottom; Jack Delano 24–5, Russell Lee 263; Gordon Parks 253 bottom; Arthur Segel 202 top, 210; John Vachon 227, 239
RDA 339
John Reekie 48–9
Jack Robinson 335 bottom left, 355 bottom
SAGA/Frank Capri 369 bottom middle
Arthur Rothstein 186, 206, 207
Santi Visalli Inc. 312 bottom
P.L. Sperr 76–7

Sporting News 254 top, 267
Scott Swanson Collection 81, 103
John Vachon 203 top
Leo Vals 348–9
Weegee Front cover, 215, 226, 253 top, 258, 259
J. N. Wilson 102
Marion Post Wolcott 222 bottom

Getty Images News and Sport

Al Bello 360–1
Clive Brunskill 365 bottom
David Cannon 366 top
Laura L. Camden 380
Manny Ceneta 342–3, 369 top
Michael Cooper 364 bottom right
Phillipe Diederich 379 top right
Tony Duffy 350, 363
Darren England 366 bottom
David Friedman 389 top
Kerry Hayes 379 top left
Chris Hondros 359 top
Chuck Kennedy 387 bottom right
Erik S. Lesser 345 top, back cover
Lawrence Lucier 375 bottom right
Clive Mason 364 bottom left
Robert Mora 379 bottom right
Doug Pensinger 364 top left
Spencer Platt 389 bottom
Mike Powell 367 top
Joe Raedle 6–7, 384
Mike Simons 388
George De Sota 379 bottom left, 383 top
Vandystadt 364 top right
Alex Wong 387 top, bottom right

Other sources

Agence France Presse 325 top, 345 bottom
The Advertising Archives 117 bottom, 347
Associated Press 340 top right; Gretchen Ertl 369 bottom left
Beinecke Rare Book and Manuscript Library, Yale University 84, 166 bottom, 194 top, 340 bottom, 341, 396
Corbis/Bettman 279 bottom
Denver Public Library 96, 97,129, 133
Detroit News Photo 250 top, 250 bottom, 251
Eakin Press 150
Gary Franklin 333, 376 bottom right
Maritime Administration USA 246 bottom
National Archives 255
Naval Historical Foundation 105
Nebraska State Historical Society 82–3
The Ohio Historical Society 116, 117 top
Robert Hunt Library 315, Charles Moore 276–7
PA Photos 368, 374, 375 top, 375 bottom left, 382; AAP 376 top; Abaca Press 371, 375 bottom middle; EPA 344, 370, 377, 378, 381, 383 bottom, 387 bottom left, 390, 391; Branimir Kvartuc 376 bottom left
Reuters 358 bottom right; Corinne Dufka 385; Michael Evstafiev 358 bottom left; Gary Hershorn 362; John Kuntz 365 top; Jeff Vinnick 346 top
Schomburg Center for Research in Black Culture, The New York Public Library, Astor, Lennox, and Tilden Foundations 85, 118 bottom, 123, 139, 155, 156, 195 top, 195 bottom, 196,197, 234, 265, 280 bottom, 290–1, 293, 298 top, 322–3; *National Geographic* 131
Phil Stern 330 top
U.S. Library of Congress 69, 106 top left, 106 bottom left, 106 bottom right, 107 top, 107 bottom left, 107 bottom right, 112 top, 112 bottom, 138, 159, 283, 158, 282, Jack Delano 223 top, 223 bottom; Marion Post Wolcott 218, 219; University of Kansas 114–15, 144 top, 145 top, 145 bottom, 146, 147
Valentine Museum/Richmond History Center 1

(Above) Children outside the New York Public Library, Schomburg Collection of Negro Literature and History in Harlem in 1965.

Index